Face Time With God

Face Time With God

GROWING IN INTIMACY WITH GOD THROUGH PRAYER & JOURNALING

MINDY BUNTING O'CONNOR

EQUIP PRESS

Colorado Springs

Face Time with God, Growing in Intimacy with God through Prayer and Journaling
Copyright © 2023 Mindy Bunting O'Connor

All rights reserved. No part of this publication may be reproduced, distributed, or transmitted in any form or by any means, without prior written permission.

Scripture quotations marked (ESV) are taken from The ESV® Bible (The Holy Bible, English Standard Version®) copyright © 2001 by Crossway, a publishing ministry of Good News Publishers. ESV® Text Edition: 2011. The ESV® text has been reproduced in cooperation with and by permission of Good News Publishers.

Unauthorized reproduction of this publication is prohibited.
Used by permission. All rights reserved.

Scripture quotations marked (KJV) are taken from the King James Bible. Accessed on Bible Gateway at www.BibleGateway.com.

Scripture quotations marked (NASB) are taken from the New American Standard Bible® (NASB), copyright © 1960, 1962, 1963, 1968, 1971, 1972, 1973, 1975, 1977, 1995 by The Lockman Foundation, www.Lockman.org. Used by permission.

Scripture quotations marked (NIV) are taken from the Holy Bible, New International Version. Copyright © 1973, 1978, 1984, 2011 by Biblica, Inc.® Used by permission. All rights reserved worldwide.

Scripture quotations marked (NKJV) are taken from the New King James Version®. Copyright © 1982 by Thomas Nelson, Inc. Used by permission. All rights reserved.

Scripture quotations marked (NLT) are taken from the Holy Bible, New Living Translation, copyright © 1996, 2004, 2015 by Tyndale House Foundation. Used by permission of Tyndale House Publishers, Inc., Carol Stream, Illinois 60188. All rights reserved.

Scripture quotations marked (NRSV) are taken from the New Revised Standard Version Bible, copyright © 1989 the Division of Christian Education of the National Scripture quotations taken from the Amplified® Bible (AMP), Copyright © 2015 by The Lockman Foundation Used by permission. www.Lockman.org

First Edition: 2023
Face Time with God / Mindy Bunting O'Connor
Paperback ISBN: 978-1-958585-47-4
eBook ISBN: 978-1-958585-48-1

ENDORSEMENT PAGE:

Dr. Charles "Chic" Shaver, Emeritus Professor of Evangelism Nazarene Theological Seminary Kansas City. Author, *Living in the Blessing*

"When I started journaling more than forty years ago, it became a major source of greater intimacy with God. Now Mindy O'Connor has come forth with a significant book about journaling. Mindy has a wonderful intimacy with God. She lives and writes in a way that welcomes you, invites you, stretches you, and grows you—but always, with this goal, you can also have an intimate relationship with God. Mindy has turned her tragedies into triumphs and will show how you can experience the same. I have known Mindy and Kevin personally. They are for real. Her book is vibrant with reality."

Kathleen Jones, Executive Director, Life Choice Pregnancy Center

"What an honor and privilege to add my name to this thoughtful, simply written outpouring of Mindy's heart and God's leading. I am truly blessed to call her a friend and sister in Christ. I love and appreciate her obedience to the Lord in writing her thoughts, prayers, and, most importantly, her survivor's story. As a director for a Pro-Life pregnancy center, her mother choosing life is the story that I fight for daily."

CHERISSE ZELESKY, SPEAKER, AND AUTHOR OF *I MISS YOU ALREADY*

"Prayer journaling is the sacred historical account of one's heart and life. Mindy O'Connor has had her share of life's interruptions, frustrations, and God-size miracles. Mindy's prayer journal speaks to all of us about the power of God's faithfulness through every season of life. This beautiful book reflects a life of knowing and trusting God. We can write our prayer journals as love letters to God and be confident He hears them. Mindy illustrates the beauty and power of writing our prayers, giving us a roadmap on how to do it. I've known Mindy for eighteen years and witnessed God unfolding her story before my eyes. I'm excited for every reader to share in this prayer journaling journey.

SANDRA H. ESCH, AUTHOR OF FOUR BOOKS: *TRACKS IN THE SNOW* **(AMBER LEAF TRILOGY BOOK 1),** *SOMEWHERE BETWEEN RAINDROPS* **(AMBER LEAF TRILOGY BOOK 2),** *A CARRIAGE RIDE HOME* **(CHRONICLES OF AMBER LEAF),** *A WHISPER ON THE WIND* **(AMBER LEAF TRILOGY BOOK 3**

In *Face Time with God*, Mindy shares thoughtful insights about her romance with God in this beautifully written, honest, and self-effacing narrative. Having coped with adoption, confusion, the untimely loss of a loved one, barrenness, and financial challenges, the struggles in her life's story offer profound hope and inspiration to those of us seeking help.

CAROLYN J. HAYS, RETIRED BUSINESS EDUCATION PROFESSOR

Over coffee, Mindy first shared one of her stories about seeking God through prayer, relying upon Him to supply her every need, and how her faith had brought about an amazing, life-changing experience. She explained this was just one of many stories she had recorded in over eighty journals she had written during the past thirty years. Eager for more, I asked if she would allow me to read a few of her journals, and she kindly consented. Immediately I recognized how her steadfast faith and total reliance upon God had resulted in incredible answers to prayer. I began calling her experiences "Mindy's Miracle Moments."

I started journaling and found that writing my thoughts and prayers supplied clarity, focus, and a renewed sense of purpose to my life. Learning from this writer's experiences, my Christian growth accelerated, and I began experiencing my own "Mindy Miracle Moments."

Like many others, I urged her to publish this book. I am delighted with this treasure trove of inspirational stories that span her lifetime of experiencing God and developing a personal relationship with Him. I highly recommend this book, trusting that you will find meaning and value in her stories and will be blessed by a newly accelerated growth in your own Christian experience.

DEDICATION

To Carolyn Hays. You came into my life as an answer to prayer! You encouraged me in my writing, held me accountable, and spent many countless hours reading my work! You believed in me and motivated me to "move to action" in sharing my "God stories" with others. "I thank my God upon every remembrance of you . . ."
(Phil. 1:3 KJV)

CONTENTS

Endorsement Page:	v
Dedication	ix
Forward	1
Action Steps to Fruitful Journaling:	2
Day Break	5
We Have Not Because We Ask Not	8
Wind and Sea	11
Threads of Time	16
Prayer Precedes Provision	20
Seek and Surrender	29
A Prayer Chair	36
Camelot	42
Christmas Wood	48
Faulty Fuel Injectors	53
Unusual Opportunity for Hospitality	57
Small as a Mustard Seed	63
Winds of Change	69
A Mighty Rushing Wind	75
My Walk to Remember	81
You Want to Read My Journals?	86
Hopelessly Romantic	92
The Blending of a Family	99
Dragonfly and a Prayer	104
Cracking the Code	109

Will You Build a Wall or a Windmill?	112
Beauty for Ashes	116
Face Time God?	120
Addendum	124
God A Quiet Company	125
About the Author	129

FORWARD

by Kevin O'Connor
Lead Pastor at The ARK Church, Redlands, California

We all are keenly aware of the sensitivity and privacy factors associated with journaling. Vulnerability comes through the sharing of personal details, including, but not limited to, emotions of joy, hurts, hopes, and disappointments. The words themselves become precious! So, who would allow others to peek into their personal life, and for what purpose? Why would someone be willing to share them? When you read the stories in this book, I can tell you firsthand you will find the answers to those questions.

This author is aware of an audience beyond herself when she writes. Her deeply personal stories are not centered around her. What she writes reveals a keen awareness of God's presence during quiet times and what she calls Face Time with God. Besides her inspiring stories, she also includes *personal dialogue with God*, written in her prayer journals over several decades. While reading her journal entries, I saw tremendous victories despite the challenges!

Mindy's stories include suspense with a different flare than expected from such narratives. Why will others want to read this book? She invites us to join her in journaling throughout the pages of this book, adding personal value to our own thoughts and prayers.

This book will challenge you to look at every area of life through a different lens. You will fall more in love with God and the author as you read her life stories! I know I did!

ACTION STEPS TO FRUITFUL JOURNALING:

Getting Started – You can begin recording your spiritual journey today. Using the lines provided in this "companion to journaling," I encourage you to write your prayers, dreams, struggles, fears, and even past failures. Write down meaningful Scriptures, quotes, and experiences. When looking for a new journal, one with lines is excellent, but if you are artsy, a book with blank pages will allow you to illustrate pages with colored pencils, markers, stickers, and photographs. I find most of my blank journals at popular discount stores. Writing out your prayers is the perfect way of documenting your relationship with God. It's also a tangible way to look back and reflect on His faithfulness, remembering the blessings when prayers were answered.

Getting a Study Bible – I have found beautiful study Bibles on Amazon! If budget is an issue, visit Goodwill or other local thrift shops. I love the New King James Version, but I have used many different translations, including the Message Bible, which paraphrases Scriptures using contemporary language. The Message is not a study Bible but a reading Bible that aims to help you read the living Word of God engagingly and intriguingly.

Surrendering – This is a safe place to give God all your frustrations and disappointments. Especially the things you feel you have no control over, by surrendering situations to God, writing out your prayers, then waiting and watching to see how He will work in and through as you trust in Him to take over. It will be a tremendous experience as you begin seeing God show up and show off in ways that only He can.

Journaling Tips – Start by dating your journal entries. Dates will be important when looking back to see how and when God answered your prayers. Write Bible passages that speak to your heart and expound on them. God will reveal more about His nature, purposes, and direction in your life as you begin to write these things from the tablets of your heart. Write about adjustments you are making. Be specific; what changes do you want God's help within your personal life? Family, finances, career, education, medical needs, or church involvement, to name a few?

Moving to Obedience – Through this fundamental principle, your romance with God will blossom! Spiritual practices include daily Scripture reading, journaling your prayers, and surrendering your life to God. If you are new to reading the Bible, start with the book of Proverbs. With thirty-one chapters, you can read one for each day of the month. God will begin revealing adjustments you can make to your lifestyle that allow His presence and power to work in and through you. God wants His character to be reflected in you so others will be drawn to Him as they see transformation in your life.

Taking Action – The wonderful, spirit-filled life is one of movement and action! Action makes the relationship come alive through praying, dreaming, shedding tears, and seeking God's help. Action is where my romance with God started! I *took action* by attending church, buying a new Bible, learning the Scriptures, journaling, and swapping old habits for new ones. God listened as I began moving, and He supernaturally rearranged situations and circumstances. Movement meant I got up on Sundays to attend church, developed a quiet time routine, read my Bible, journaled my prayers, and attended small group Bible studies.

Experience Sacrifice – Sacrificing something valuable or important means giving it up to obtain something for yourself or someone you love. Jesus' sacrifice on the cross is how God saved humankind from sin and death. On the first day of January 2023, I vowed to give up Facebook until after Easter. That time I spent mindlessly scrolling through Facebook, I would spend mindfully scrolling through the scriptures, spending more time with God, and seeking greater ways to honor Him with my time. Giving up Facebook for Face Time with God is when this book was supernaturally jumpstarted right before my eyes.

Your sacrifice could be an old lifestyle, or something you mindlessly do that separates you from time spent with God. It might be giving up entertainment that draws you away from God instead of closer to Him. Maybe your sacrifice is simply trading your unbelief toward belief in God so He can direct you to better things (friends, employment, and financial breakthroughs).

> "My sacrifice, O God, is a broken spirit;
> a broken and contrite heart, O God, you
> will not despise." (Ps. 51:17 NIV)

DAY BREAK

"Let all that I am wait quietly before God, for my hope is in Him. He alone is my rock and my salvation . . ." (Ps. 62:5–6 NLT)

As written in my journal dated July 28, 2009:

It's been a while since I've felt the closeness with God that I've been feeling lately. After moving to a new town, becoming a blended family and a pastor's wife, I have felt like a woman with a "Mary" heart, trapped in a "Martha" lifestyle. The ordinary life of simplicity I once enjoyed had cultivated an extraordinary relationship with God! That part of me seemed to be left behind when my life drastically changed. In those days, I prioritized God, giving Him the best of my attention, enthusiasm, and energy. During those simpler days, it seemed I had a direct lifeline within the secret places of my heart where God dwelled. Today there are so many things demanding to come first, vying for my time and energy. Father, I come to you today eagerly anticipating more of you in my life here.

One day later, on July 29, 2009:

This morning I was awakened by God's Spirit at 4 a.m. with a song stuck in my head from last night's Prayer and Praise service. The song kept playing in my mind like an alarm clock waking me before anyone else was up. Though I tried, I could not fall back to sleep. I decided to get up and spend that time in God's Word. (Had I stayed in bed, I would have missed a fantastic God opportunity!)

Stepping into my soft slippers beside the bed, I tiptoed to the kitchen to make hot tea. As I laid my Bible on the table, I noticed an ominously dark sky through the breakfast nook's bay window. I was drawn outside to look more closely at the early morning sky above me. It was still too dark to distinguish different objects but illuminated enough for me to see the mystical display of clouds in the heavenlies! What I was experiencing was that magical moment called twilight !

I was about to realize this wouldn't be just an ordinary day! Knowing my small camera wouldn't capture the intensity of the daybreak, cloud-filled sky, I grabbed another cup of steaming hot tea and headed to my prayer chair to journal another God experience.

I opened my all-time favorite devotional book, *My Utmost for His Highest*, by Oswald Chambers. A black satin ribbon marked the spot of that day's reading. Opening to July 29, I realized this would have been Tom's fifty-third birthday. Tom and I were high school sweethearts, and we had been happily married for twenty-six years. After staring at the majestic clouds I had awakened to that morning, I was absolutely astonished to read the heading of that day's devotional, dated July 29: *What Do You See in Your Clouds?* "Behold, He cometh with clouds . . ." (Rev. 1:7 KJV) Continuing to read, Oswald said that clouds are always connected with God in the Bible! Chambers goes on to say that there is a connection between the strange providential circumstances allowed by God and what we can know of Him. "The clouds are but the dust of our Father's feet. A sign that God is there!" (Nah. 1:3)

I could hardly believe what I was reading, realizing that God had intentionally woken me up early that morning because He wanted to spend time with me. He was revealing His splendor in the heavenly realm while painting a picture in the sky of the darkness, fleeing the light!

When God is in your life, He will get involved in every aspect! Even if you are asleep! Could it be possible God wants to woo you to himself today? I've provided spaces so you can begin journaling today. Don't worry about penmanship and spelling! This is the start of your story of growing in intimacy with God! I thank Him in advance for what He will reveal to you through His Word and Spirit.

> "But what happens when we live God's way? He brings gifts into our lives, much like fruit appears in an orchard—things like affection for others, exuberance about life, and serenity." (Gal. 5:22 Message)

ACTION STEP: Begin to record your spiritual journey on the lines provided throughout:

WE HAVE NOT BECAUSE WE ASK NOT

"I can do all things through Christ who strengthens me." (Phil. 4:13 NKJV)

Scripture reminds us God won't withhold any good thing from us. Prayer is a privilege God has given to us so we can talk with Him. How can we blame God when things fall apart if we have neglected to seek His wisdom and direction regarding the things taking place?

An undeniable power comes through praying, praising, and confessing. You may not feel like praying or aren't sure you even know how to pray. Prayer is simply spending time with God, acknowledging your needs and fears, then praising Him for His work in your situation. If you've done things you know have not been pleasing to God, confess that to Him and turn away from what has had you in bondage.

Prayer is one area where I don't feel rushed, misunderstood, or judged. It slows me down, allowing me time to reflect on the people I love and the good things that come through prayer. The stories in this book come from the pure delight I have experienced as my prayers were answered. The following is an example of a simple childlike prayer I journaled more than twenty-seven years ago during a financially challenging time, and what happened next.

Journal Entry - March 24th, 1996:

God, I need to make a little money. Making twenty dollars would help pay for Hannah's dance lesson or allow me to take her somewhere fun for lunch.

During Bible Study that day, I learned that we have little because we ask for little (James 4:3 NKJV). Later in the day, I journaled: *God, all I asked for was twenty dollars . . . maybe I should have asked for a little more. LOL.*

What happened next? My mom stopped by my house to give me a fifteen-dollar gift certificate to get Hannah something new and gave us an ice cream coupon for Baskin-Robbins! The next thing I knew, my phone rang, and the associate pastor at our church asked if I would do some typing for him! He said he had about five hours of typing and offered to pay me. I had asked God for twenty dollars and was blessed with seventy-five! I had asked to make money. In answer to that prayer, I made money through typing, and my needs were met above and beyond.

ACTION STEP: Is there something you need today? Write your prayer here and date it. Then watch to see what God will do on your behalf.

WIND AND SEA

"The wind blows wherever it pleases. You hear its sound, but you cannot tell where it comes from or where it is going. So it is with everyone born of the Spirit." (John 3:8 NIV)

While working for a flight school in the quaint college town of San Luis Obispo, I benefited from working with some of the funniest, most motivated young pilots! I also got to take free flying lessons from enthusiastic pilots needing more flight hours to become commercial airline pilots!

My flight instructor and I would squeeze into a two-seater Cessna 152, gently lifting off the runway and soaring over the beautiful, sparsely populated coastal range of the Santa Lucia Mountains and the Pacific Ocean's sandy beaches. The views were spectacular, especially on sunny days flying over the Big Sur Highway, Point Lobos, Mission San Antonio, Monterey, San Simeon, and Hearst Castle.

Recently a photo of a bright-orange windsock caught my attention while surfing the internet. The caption beneath it read: *As the winds of change blow, do you lean in and fight, or do you harness the change and sail off on an adventure?* What a great question!

Having become a newlywed and moving from the hometown I'd grown up in, I quickly experienced significant changes in every area of my life. I joyfully embraced the changes and was very optimistic about my new future. I was learning what it was to be a young wife, manage a home, find new employment, and learn my way around a new area before such a thing as GPS. Learning to fly was definitely me harnessing change and sailing off on an exciting new adventure!

The winds of change come to everyone. But not everyone knows how to embrace them. With some changes, life becomes instantly more exciting! Others, however, require stronger faith and greater perseverance! Now in the autumn of my life, I look back and see how intricately God was involved in every change. Truly He was working all things together for good!

Moving to San Luis Obispo and landing a job at the airport brought many new friendships and experiences! Craig Hutain was a twenty-two-year-old aviator that loved the thrill of doing gravity-defying tricks that made even the birds envious. I remember the exhilaration of flying with him in a two-seater, open-cockpit biplane called a Pitts Special. The small, lightweight plane was painted in bright colors that more resembled something seen in an amusement park than in an airport! Upon takeoff, it was like a rocket going straight up in the air! Once we reached the proper altitude, Craig began doing aerobatic maneuvers more thrilling than any roller coaster. Midair maneuvers had me flying upside down over the deep blue ocean with only a four-point harness to keep me from falling out! Our first two midair stunts were simple rolls and loops.

Next, Craig, being the instructor that he was, pointed out that a spin is more complex than a roll and he was more than happy to demonstrate by intentionally stalling a wing causing the plane to descend and spiral like a corkscrew.

Next was the hammerhead, also known as a stall turn, which is performed by pulling the aircraft up until it points straight up, continuing until the airspeed drops to a critical point, turning 180 degrees, and the plane pointing straight down. At the same time, the plane gained speed but traveled in the opposite direction from where the maneuver began. That's when I yelled, "Take me down!" I was ready to be safely back on the ground, but it was the thrill of a lifetime.

While writing this chapter, I heard the sad news that Craig Hutain was in one of the planes that collided midair and crashed during the Wings Over Dallas airshow on November 12, 2022. News articles said Craig died loving what he did. He will be missed.

Today I'm more down to earth! I'm a pastor's wife, grandma, stepmom, and international host mom. I've done some adventuresome things, but my faith journey has proved to be the most exciting! It all started after walking into a small church in San Luis Obispo on a random Sunday night. A coworker named Jan had invited me to an evening church service that became the life-changing catalyst that brought me to where I am today.

One of the flight instructors my friend Jan and I worked with knew she was going through a painful divorce, and he invited us to his church. That evening when we walked into the small church, Mr. Trimmer almost fell off his chair. It was a small group of strangers, but I wholeheartedly accepted Jesus as my Lord and Savior! As we talked about my new commitment to Christ, Mr. Trimmer mentioned baptism as the next step in my new faith walk. I said, "I want to be baptized tonight!" The pastor seemed totally caught off guard, warning me the water in the baptistery wouldn't be warm. My reply was, "That's okay. I swim in the ocean."

I left that small church a much different person than when I walked in. It marked the beginning of a fresh, clean start. When I arrived home with wet hair, my young husband, Tom, asked about why my hair was wet, knowing I had planned to attend a church service that night. I was radiating my new joy found in Christ. When I told him I had been baptized, he slid down the leather couch in one smooth move, leaning back as if he were seeing a ghost. He had no choice at that point; I was all in, and he watched in amazement as the old Mindy was gone and the new was very much alive.

Becoming a Christian is the most profound life-changing experience a person can have. Looking back, I realize that I had harnessed the wind that night! When referring to God, the Hebrew word "Ruach" means *breath*, *wind*, or a *life force that sustains all living things* (Gen. 1:2). Understanding this helps us better know who and what God is. It's God's Spirit living inside us that sustains us.

I love the creativity of God's work in an individual's life; it is awe-inspiring. Throughout my writing I will share personal details of my life openly and honestly. If you have not yet discovered the rich treasure found in the Scriptures, I am praying you will be encouraged to dig deeper after reading my stories of faith.

Initially, I began journaling my prayers to leave a spiritual legacy for my children and grandchildren. (The handwritten stories of God's work in my life.) From time to time, I'll reread my personal prayer journals of yesteryear, and I'm amazed at how God's hand was miraculously weaving together each experience in my life. Much like my grandmother did when she created patchwork quilts from fabric scraps too insignificant for anything else. Small fabric pieces cut from old clothes and flour sacks gained new purpose and became one-of-a-kind works of art. No single quilt was ever the same. Each piece connected, stitched in time and handed down to her children's children.

When the winds of change blow, will you be ready to harness the change? What do you need God's help with? Friendships, faith, strength, healing? Possibly new employment or a place to live or church to attend? Perhaps it's time you harness the winds of change and sail off on a new adventure with the God of the universe!

> "He caused an east wind to blow in the heaven:
> and by his power, he brought in the south wind."
> (Ps. 78:26 KJV)

ACTION STEP: How might you harness the winds of change today, trusting God to guide you?

THREADS OF TIME

"So teach us to number our days that we may get a heart of wisdom." (Ps. 90:12 KJV)

Growing up adopted, I often wondered who I looked like. Never having met my biological father, all I knew were the few things my mom had been willing to share. She told me my father's family was from Portugal, and I had his eyes. Natural curiosity made me want to learn more though it was a taboo subject rarely mentioned. Occasionally I would pry, but once when I did, I detected pain in my mother's eyes. I had asked her to tell me about him, and there was a quick flash of anger in her blue eyes. She said: "I don't know why you want to know about him? He didn't want to know anything about you!" The subject was dropped.

I became an avid young observer and listener when Mom or Aunty mentioned anything about my biological family or their small town near Santa Barbara. I found the names she had written in my baby book at birth and the legal adoption papers that had been signed when I was almost five. Like many adopted children, I secretly dreamed I might meet these people someday. I imagined myself smelling and tasting their Portuguese cooking and what it would be like to experience their traditions and celebrations. Things like linguica, kale soup, and sweet bread sounded so delicious! I wondered if they loved gardening like I did. Did they love spicy foods?

Mom ended up falling in love with a handsome, young police officer. They were married when I was four, and he wanted to legally adopt me. He became my first knight in shining armor. I was so excited to have a daddy, and I still remember that day at the courthouse when I became his daughter.

After becoming a Christian, I began to pray about this disconnect in my life. Naturally, I assumed my bio father had met another woman he had wanted to start a family with. Was I his well-kept secret, or did his new family know of me? I didn't want him or his family to be hurt by hearing about me, and I didn't want to hurt the "dad" who had chosen to raise me. I wondered, could my selfish desires to know them, negatively affect others just so I could know where I came from? My greatest fear in looking for them sooner was the fear of being rejected.

After two cancer diagnoses in 2010, missing medical history would have been helpful information for me to have. Every time throughout my life, when I was asked to fill out medical forms, I always had to leave one side blank. At fifty-six, I prayerfully decided to Google my Portuguese family's name. In minutes I found who I believed was a family member. Before sending a quick email to who I thought might possibly be a sister, I bowed my head at the computer and prayed before hitting the send button.

After several days, I received the following reply in large bold print: "Mindy, we are related! I'm your first cousin! You have two brothers and a huge Portuguese family! Unfortunately, I'm sorry to say your biological father passed away some years ago."

Brothers? I have brothers. Though I would never meet the man Mom said I got my green eyes from, I felt like I met him the day I met and embraced both my brothers! That was an exciting year, and another prayer had been answered! Soon after meeting my brothers, they invited me to their family reunion, where I also met aunties, whose names had been written in my baby book fifty-six years earlier. What an amazing answer to prayer. Never underestimate what God will do on your behalf when you trust Him.

The night of the family reunion, my brothers took me from table to table, introducing me to two-hundred aunts, uncles, and cousins! To most of them, I was a complete and total surprise. To several, I was the face of a long-kept family secret. One cousin exclaimed, "How did a family this big keep a secret like this for so long?" We laughed, hugged, savored flavorful foods, and shared our life stories with each other around the different tables. A night I'll never forget.

The oldest aunt, whom I was told might be the most difficult, seemed to have dementia when I was first introduced to her. She sat quietly. The rejection I feared was detected there momentarily, but it was okay. Somehow, I understood her pain. I had stepped into her world, and she hadn't expected to see me there.

Toward the end of the evening, I was standing by an exit door, and I could see her slowly approaching me. She held her hand out to me and said, "It's nice to meet you, Mindy; welcome to the family." I felt like I had won the lottery! One of the matriarchs in the family extended her hand of grace to me, and I am so grateful for having met her.

ACTION STEP: Write about something you have been dreaming about that would take God to get it done.

PRAYER PRECEDES PROVISION

". . . and walk in the way of love, just as Christ loved us and gave himself up for us as a fragrant offering and sacrifice to God." (Eph. 5:2 NIV)

Provision of God's people is a prevalent theme throughout the Bible. When the Israelites wandered forty years in the desert, God miraculously supplied bread/manna from heaven each day. The Gospels describe how Jesus took just two fish and five small loaves of bread, blessed them, and fed a multitude of people! (Daily bread needs.)

We also know Jesus miraculously turned water into wine at a wedding in Cana. Interestingly, wine hasn't been made instantly or supernaturally by anyone other than Jesus. Wine takes time to ferment! Jesus demonstrated that he could bypass time as we know it and simply turn water into wine. No grapes. No winepress. No aging processes. No wine yeast or sugar. Instantly he created what the Bible said was the best wine. When we read the Scriptures, we see a common thread that connects our prayers with God's provisions, and He has no limitations in accomplishing what He desires to take place.

I recently read that it would require at least thirty-two pounds of grapes to make one gallon or approximately five bottles of wine! One ceremonial water jar in Jesus' day could hold twenty to thirty gallons. My math is not good, but it looks as though Jesus instantly made somewhere between 120 and 180 gallons of wine! That is some provision! By today's standards, that would have been enough to fill approximately 750 to 1,000 wine bottles, just to get a modern-day perspective.

Before my daughter turned three, I prayed she would be able to attend Christian school when she entered kindergarten. When the time came to enroll her in school, we were the least likely family to send our child to a private school.

When I was growing up, many of my friends aspired to become

accountants, teachers, or Olympians. From a young age, I knew I wanted to be *a keeper of the home.* After becoming a mom, I knew it was what I wanted to be. I wasn't opposed to women working outside the house, but it wasn't my personal vision for our family. I vowed to live more simply to help make that desire come to pass. I was dreaming and envisioning the simple life long before tiny homes and fixer-uppers were a thing.

During my years of infertility, I found comfort and inspiration in reading stories about women in the Bible who had known the pain of longing for a child: Hannah, Rebecca, Rachel, Sarah, and Elizabeth each struggled with barrenness. Their fervent prayers were heard by God and answered somewhat miraculously. Their faith inspired me.

Each of these women went on to have sons who became faithful men of God. Isaac, the only son of Sarah and Abraham, was promised to them in their old age. Sarah was so old she laughed at the thought of being pregnant at such an advanced age. Abraham was 100 years old when their son was born. They raised Isaac, and he obeyed God and followed His commands.

Rachel was a faithful wife to Jacob. She gave birth to Benjamin, and Joseph, who became one of the most important figures of the Old Testament, saving the nation of Israel during a famine. Joseph became one of the twelve tribes of Israel and was known as "the righteous one." His father had favored him, and his jealous brothers sold him as a slave to Egypt, where he ultimately became ruler of the land, second only to King Pharaoh.

Elizabeth was the mother of John the Baptist and the wife of Zechariah. According to the Gospel of Luke, she also was past the average childbearing age when she conceived and gave birth to John. The angel Gabriel announced to Zechariah that he would have a son. Gabriel said about John: "He will be great in the sight of the Lord. He will be filled with the Holy Spirit even before he is born. He will bring many of Israel's people to the Lord their God."

True to the word of the Lord, Zechariah's wife, Elizabeth, gave birth to John. Zechariah said: "You, my child, will be called a prophet of the Highest; for you will go on before the Lord to prepare the way for Him." What a great reminder of God's purpose and timing. When God has a plan and a purpose for your life, He also has the ideal time to bring it to pass.

If Elizabeth had conceived in her time frame, her son, John the Baptist, wouldn't have been born six months before Jesus to prepare the way for the Messiah! God could have chosen a younger, more fertile couple. Still, to show his unlimited grace and power, God sent this harbinger (a person or thing that announces or signals the approach of another) of our Lord through a God-honoring couple past their prime. The name John, which Zechariah and Elizabeth chose for their son, means "the grace of God."

The Bible doesn't specifically say how long Hannah was barren, but many believe her infertility lasted nineteen years (Prov. 17:3 NIV). "The crucible for silver and a furnace for gold, but the Lord tests the heart." God refines the righteous according to their strength; He refined Sarah for twenty-five years, Rebecca for twenty, and Hannah for nineteen.

If you or someone you know has struggled to conceive, you understand the depth of these women's sorrow. For so many years, I thought infertility was what defined these women's lives. No, it was their faith in God that defined them. What is it you may wrongly feel has defined you? Do you believe God can change your life miraculously? Why or why not? Is anything too difficult for God?

Do infertile women still conceive and give birth today without fertility drugs? Yes, I am one of them. My prayers were answered after a long time of waiting faithfully. Those years of infertility became essential to my spiritual pilgrimage.

I would read the book of Psalms and find it perplexing that God told barren Sarah she would "become a mother to many and be a joyful mother to her children." (Ps. 113:9 KJV). Today I understand that Scripture better, for I, too, have become a mother to many.

Is there something you've been praying for, wondering if God hears? I wish I could say I had been patiently content during my years of infertility, but I was frustrated and confused. Yet my faith during those years grew exponentially! God's purpose was to create in me a heart that loved Him because one day, He would trust me with much more than a child. He would use me to minister beyond my own four walls and neighborhood. He would allow me to be a mother of many, though only one child would be "flesh of my flesh, bone of my bone." Looking back, I see God's graciousness in giving my husband Tom and me a fourteen-year honeymoon! We had assumed we would be the couple that grew old together, but that would not be the case.

Not wanting to be a bitter or complaining wife, my heart's plea became, "God, what do you want for my life?" In Proverbs 31, the worthy woman isn't so concerned with the appearance of circumstances. Instead, she focuses on God's truth, believing in His provision.

When it came time to enroll my daughter, Hannah, in kindergarten, I had only two choices: Enroll her in public school, where her education would cost us nothing, or choose a Christian school, which needed immediate upfront payment for registration, and ongoing monthly tuition payments. One choice seemed easy, while the other would require much faith and sacrifice! It was prayerfully decided; Hannah would attend Christian school. We were moving to a new level of faith. The kind that develops spiritual maturity.

We were learning to understand more of who God is and developing a greater awareness of His presence daily. Working in tandem with God meant we had "skin in the game." Instead of buying new clothes and shoes, I shopped in thrift stores and gladly took others' hand-me-downs. Our humble home didn't have a dishwasher, a garage, or air conditioning. But it was paid for, which was all in God's perfect timing and provision.

When grocery shopping, I carried a calculator, returning items to the shelf when I reached my budget (cash in my wallet). I gave up luxuries like getting my nails done, cable TV, internet, and a cellphone. Ironically as our material possessions decreased, God seemed to increase! Having more time than money allowed us to help many others, serving in our church, community, school, and neighborhood. Our sacrifices were becoming a *fragrant offering*! (Phil. 4:18). We were becoming rich in things money couldn't buy.

For Christians, faith is not blind. It is confident. "Now faith is confidence in what we hope for and assurance about what we do not see." (Heb 11:1 NIV) Hope only acknowledges things might improve. But hope in God believes divine intervention will bring changes that work together for good. Not everything that happens is good, but we have the promise that God will work it together for good to those who love Him and are called according to His purpose.

My daughter started kindergarten, and teachers were eager for parents to sign up as classroom volunteers on back-to-school night. I signed up that night to work in Mrs. Lorah's kindergarten classroom. Four months later, the school offered me a part-time job with a significant tuition discount, which saw Hannah through the eighth grade! Still, another miracle would one day come, opening the door for her to attend Pt. Loma Nazarene University in San Diego when it came time for her to enter college. God continued to honor the prayers I prayed so long ago. Isn't it great to know our prayers don't have expiration dates? Prayers from twenty, thirty, or forty years still get answered, often when and how we least expect it.

Skipping ahead, Hannah was a college student at PLNU and had been home for the summer. She and I were having one of our mother-daughter talks on the patio when I told her, "California no longer allows parents or students to pay for education using credit cards. We have a significant payment due before you can register for fall classes. "We have to pray."

My phone began ringing no sooner than I said those words. It was someone from the Christian high school here in Redlands. They were given our name as a reference for possibly hosting two international students from China. One was in ninth grade, and the other was a tenth grader. They were already en route to America. If their plane landed in the United States without a host family address, they would be sent back to China on the next plane leaving LAX. They needed a family ASAP. As much as I wanted to help these girls and the school, I honestly didn't know how we could take on added expenses with two more in our home. I told the school we would pray about it. She said to pray quickly because she needed an answer that day. We said, "Yes."

The students being in two different grades would mean different schedules, requiring two or three daily trips to and from the school, ten miles from our Yucaipa home. The school explained that there would be a small stipend to help with expenses, but we were leaning toward doing it either way. We loved the idea of our home becoming an extension of our ministry life. What an excellent opportunity to share our faith and unconditional love with young girls from a country whose government churches are basically run by atheists.

That afternoon the school came to do a home inspection and began a background check on us. Two days later, two timid Chinese girls arrived at our door. They were wearing backpacks backward, which I later learned was to prevent pickpocketing in China. They were tired and just meeting us for the first time, and my heart went out to them. I loved them already!

Imagine our surprise when the school handed us an envelope with a cash stipend tucked inside to help with each girl's room and board for the fall semester. I won't say how much it was, but it paid what we owed immediately to Pt. Loma University! It also paid our due property taxes and gave our girls a most memorable first Christmas and school year. Two girls entered our hearts and home that day. Through the years, that international program helped make me a mother to many. Over the past eleven years, we have continued hosting students from China, Vietnam, Africa, and Korea! More than twelve international students have called us "Mom and Dad." Some continue to come "home" for holidays and special occasions, and it blesses our hearts. There are no limits to what God will do if you are willing to participate.

ACTION STEP: Is there something you are willing to give up (sacrifice) as a sweet fragrance to God? Time, talent, resources? Maybe a bedroom?

From an Old Journal Entry:

Heavenly Father, please multiply our resources, energy . . . and benefits. My heart desires great things, but who am I to ask such things? Your Word says I am your daughter, an heir. Everything you own will one day be mine. You are my Father, my friend, and my teacher. Your love for me has made me the woman I am today. Your love and forgiveness have allowed me to let go of things in my past that could have destroyed me. Instead, I'm on a new path, excited and ready to serve. Lead me and teach me in the ways of righteousness, truth, and spiritual growth. Amen.

SEEK AND SURRENDER

"God did this so that they would seek him and perhaps reach out for him and find him, though he is not far from any one of us." (Acts 17:27 NIV)

My biological clock had been ticking, and I was learning the virtue of patience/waiting on the Lord. When motherhood hadn't come naturally within my time frame, I took matters into my own hands. If Tom and I could not conceive a child, surely God wanted to fulfill our heart's desire through adoption. We contacted an adoption attorney in Santa Barbara, and his ability to match us with a birth mom was expedient! We were chosen by a young girl who was unmarried, pregnant, and with a two-year-old to care for. She felt placing her child in a Christian home was the most loving thing she could do. She had read our personal bio page and was anxious to meet us. We shared our hopes and dreams with her, and she shared her dreams for the child she was carrying.

February was a perfect month to fall in love with this young girl who was choosing us to love and raise the child she was carrying. Her baby being due June 30 gave us plenty of time to get to know her and prepare for the new and exciting days ahead. I enjoyed getting to know her and saw this as a great opportunity to encourage and disciple her new faith. As her due date quickly approached, I gave my notice at work, and friends showered me with gifts. I found a beautiful wicker crib with small drawers for storing baby's outfits, bibs, and blankets, and it all felt like a beautiful dream!

On the evening of June 24, the phone call we anxiously anticipated came. We jumped in the car and excitedly drove to San Clemente Hospital to pray and wait.

At last, a nurse came to the waiting area to tell us a healthy baby girl had been born. We gowned up, and when they placed her in my arms, I thought she was the most beautiful baby I had ever seen, with her little button nose, long, dark hair, and pink rosebud lips. We hated leaving her at the hospital that night but promised to return first thing the following morning. I hardly slept that night, knowing my arms would no longer be empty. Morning couldn't come quickly enough, and as soon as the sun was up, I sprang out of bed—which I'm not known for doing.

Our phone rang just before we were ready to walk out the door. Tom answered and listened quietly, and then I heard him say, "Would you please tell Mindy?" It was our attorney. That call was one every adoptive couple most fears. Our birth mom had changed her mind. The nursery would remain empty, and I would return to the job I had resigned from two weeks earlier.

The days that followed left us feeling as if our baby had died, but sadly we didn't have the peace of knowing she was in a better place. I returned to work, and each morning, my Nazarene neighbor, Maxine Vail, would open her front door, hug me, and say a simple prayer over me. She knew a dark shadow of depression had fallen on me like a cold, dark mist. The Vails were such a comfort to us during that difficult time. When we told them the sad news, they fasted and prayed for me for three days! They showed us what it looked like to love our neighbor, and we were blessed to know them. How they came to be our next-door neighbors, is another God story, for another time.

Tom and I had been married for thirteen years, and sadly our nest remained empty. It was time for me to wave the white flag. I wasn't giving up; I was at long last surrendering my will to God. Submitting to God's authority meant I needed to yield, relent, give up, and abandon myself entirely. Lifting my hands to heaven one morning, I began waving my invisible white flag. At that very moment, I accepted my life from that day forward according to God's will. With hands still raised, I said aloud, "God, if you could give up your only Son for me, I will give up my desire for a son or a daughter for you. But God, you put this love in my heart for children; please do not waste it. Show me how I can be a vessel you might use. Can I work for a school? Open a daycare? Lord, show me the path you have laid out for me."

I cannot explain the relief I experienced that day! The dreams of conceiving ended. Thoughts of adoption fled. I was joyfully dreaming of new ways God might use me to share my love with other people's children. I dreamed of buying a small house to operate a daycare. I would call it "Our House." I imagined the excitement of kids raising pets and climbing trees! I visualized a white picket fence surrounded by fragrant flowers and veggie gardens. I could almost hear the laughter and excitement of kids planting seeds and watching them grow.

I wanted God to see I was fully surrendered to His will and waiting for His leading. This was a new level of living out my faith in obedience! The baby things in the garage rafters no longer loomed overhead as a dark and painful reminder of loss. I decided I would sell those things to someone that could use them. Having already sold the stroller and cloth diapers, I had someone scheduled to look at the crib. The morning they were coming to see it, I rescheduled for another weekend, assuming I had a stomach bug.

At this same time, I had been interviewing for a new job and assured them we weren't pursuing adoption. I got the job, and two weeks later, my coworkers gave me a nice going-away lunch. The men in the office gave me beautiful, long-stemmed red roses, and the girls handed me a mysterious, gift-wrapped box to open when I got home.

The gift the ladies had given me was an early pregnancy test kit! I had been so tired that last week at work, they speculated I might be pregnant. The directions on the box said it could accurately detect pregnancy before a missed menstrual cycle, so when I got home, Tom did the chemistry while I arranged the roses in a tall, crystal vase. I walked into our bedroom with the vase of roses, and Tom looked at me with one eyebrow raised and said, "According to this, it's definitely positive!"

I started to laugh! Then the tears began to flow. We sat momentarily on the edge of the bed, completely stunned. I was pregnant after thirteen years of marriage? It hadn't even occurred to us that I might be pregnant. The "stomach bug" I experienced must have been a wave of morning sickness. How would I tell my new employer Monday morning? I had assured them we would not be starting a family.

I made an appointment with a doctor to confirm what we already suspected. He looked at me and said, "Congratulations, you are pregnant. Your due date is June 30." Coincidentally, June 30 was our birth mom's due date precisely three years prior.

On a hot summer night before my thirty-fifth birthday, Tom and I had a beautiful daughter placed in our arms, and we named her Hannah. Remember the perplexing question from Psalm 113:9, where the barren woman becomes a mother to many? I understand that Scripture so well today because I have been a mother to many. Even though I gave birth to only one child, God opened doors allowing me to share my love with so many more. Remember my prayer asking God if I could work in a school? God opened a door for me to work nine years at a Christian school, and I loved it. Remember me asking God if I could open a daycare? I had the joy of spending eight summers doing daycare in my home. "Our House" was a place where kids built tree forts, raised critters, ate vine-ripened tomatoes, and served lunches and teas in my rustic garden with the white picket fence.

Families from Christian schools, churches, and neighborhoods would pay to enjoy our homemade specialties at our Garden Café. Some of our favorite menu items included clam chowder in sourdough bowls, garden spaghetti made with veggies we grew, Zorba Sandwiches, broccoli cheese soup, grilled sourdough, ham and cheese sandwiches. Those were memory-making moments with so many children.

Tom and I didn't get to adopt the sweet little girl with the pink rosebud lips, but we were able to help lead her teenage mom into a relationship with Jesus. She was one of the first people I called when I discovered I was pregnant. I have never heard someone cry for another's happiness as she did that day for mine.

I hope this story has touched your heart in a personal way. Perhaps you have a longing not yet fulfilled: marriage, education, family, or possibly publishing your own book? If you have prayed to no avail, it might be time to wave the white flag and surrender your will. God will not waste an opportunity to bring something good out of something challenging.

> "And without faith, it is impossible to please Him,
> for he who comes to God must believe that He is a
> rewarder of those who seek Him." (Heb. 11:6 NKJV)

ACTION STEP: What have you been holding on to that you could surrender to God's will?

From an Old Journal Entry:

Dear Heavenly Father,

Today as I journal my prayers, I trust that my faith will not be in vain and that you, God, will be glorified in my life. Help me when I am weak to be strong. Help me when I doubt, to see you turn my doubt into faith. Help me to know your peace that passes understanding. Help me to love you on a newer and more profound level. Bless our family and see us through times of trial and uncertainty; I pray and thank you for your everlasting love. I pray you can use this experience from my life for others to see how you work all things together for good. In the precious name of Jesus our Savior, Amen

A PRAYER CHAIR

"Look! It's Solomon's sedan chair, with sixty of the best soldiers in Israel surrounding it." (Song of Solomon 3:7 ISV)

The royal blue, wingback chair that sits snugly in the corner of my bedroom may be old by most people's standards, but it's still my favorite chair. Beside it sits an antique, nineteenth-century, mahogany bookcase I found at an antique store twenty-nine years ago. Behind the triple glass doors are approximately ninety of my handwritten prayer journals.

If this blue chair could talk, the stories it would tell! Before having its prominent spot in the master bedroom, it was in our home office. But before that, it had been in the small living room of my Visalia house, where it first came to be called my prayer chair.

The first time I saw this chair it was in the corner of a Goodwill store. I had been praying for a comfortable chair, so as soon as I saw it, I knew it was an answer to my prayers. Living on a tight, sometimes non-existent budget meant praying for everything. I can't tell you how often supernatural provision resulted from my simple, childlike prayers.

My husband, Tom, had back problems, and our recliner chair was unsupportive. Replacement with a better-functioning chair was not an option financially speaking, so I prayed to find another chair that wouldn't cause Tom painful back spasms.

I don't know if you have ever been that tight financially, but if you have, you understand the need to pray for everything. Most people I knew shopped at furniture stores when they needed a new chair. I shopped at garage sales and thrift stores. Everything from appliance parts to home decor—the Goodwill, Emergency Aid, and Rescued Treasures would mysteriously have precisely what I needed when I needed it.

The first thing I saw as I walked through the doors of Goodwill that afternoon was this beautiful, royal blue wingback chair. I was pretty familiar with thrift store furniture, and at once, I knew this chair was special. It had just been donated, and they hadn't had a chance to put a price on it. I had just cashed my check and had a hundred dollars cash in my wallet—which was a miracle in and of itself! I quickly found the store manager, who said, "How about a hundred and fifty dollars?" That was a high-priced item on my budget!

I sat in the chair, praying silently. The manager could tell I really wanted it. He explained that it was well worth the price, with which I had to agree, but I only had one-hundred dollars. I might not be able to buy it, but nobody else could buy if I was sitting in it. I finally asked if there was any way he would sell it to me for what I had. Surprisingly, he said he would, and I could hardly contain my joy.

Thirty minutes later, Tom backed his truck up to load my newest thrift store bargain. I told him, "It looks like one of those expensive Lane-type chairs." Noticing it was also a reclining chair, Tom agreed it seemed a great buy. He was especially impressed with how it supported his lower back. I was so excited I beat him home to quickly make room for our new chair.

From the look on his face when he got home, my worst fear was it had fallen out of his pickup in transit. He told me the neck pillow had flipped up in the wind, and he had something I had to see. My heart sank, expecting the worst. With the cushion flipped upside down, the underside of the chair exposed the Lane Furniture logo. Stapled beneath the reclining footrest was the plastic-covered manufacturer's warranty! It was a brand-new chair that could have sold for six or seven-hundred dollars! It fit perfectly where the old rocker recliner had been and quickly became everyone's favorite chair.

Each morning I would sit in that chair with my Bible, journaling and praying for my list of people who had requested prayer. As the head of the prayer chain at our church, I had a binder to keep track of who I was praying for and a tab where I recorded praise reports as God miraculously touched and healed people's afflictions. My husband was on that list, too ... Unfortunately, he would not receive the healing his body needed this side of eternity. When his cancer made getting him in and out of a bathtub difficult, hospice showed me how to bathe him while sitting in my prayer chair. I bathed him in prayer with soothing aloes and oils.

Toward the end of Tom's illness, he slept long hours on the couch and then in a hospital bed after it was delivered. I spent many long afternoons and evenings in my prayer chair, reading my Bible and praying for God's strength and peace. From cover to cover, I read, underlined, and copied the sacred Scriptures that were carrying me through "to death do us part."

Since those days, so long ago, I have also prayed for the new man God brought into my life after losing Tom. In that chair, I have prayed for the birth of all our grandchildren and still do today. Paisley loves for me to sit in my chair telling her Bible stories. She loves me to tell her family stories of people she won't meet on this side of eternity: Grandpa Tom, Great Aunty, and Great-Great Grandma Violet. As you might think, I have fought a few battles and shed quite a few tears in that chair.

In the Kendrick Brothers movie, *The War Room*, Elizabeth (played by Priscilla Shirer) was becoming bitter and beginning to crumble under the strain of a failing marriage. Elizabeth's life took an unexpected turn for the better when she met her newest client, Miss Clara (Karen Abercrombie), who encouraged the couple to learn how prayer changes situations and circumstances. The term "War Room" stems from the military efforts during WW1 and WWII. The first war room used in 1901 was located at a military headquarters. Leaders and strategists would meet in the war room to discuss their strategies to win the war. Elizabeth's closet became her "War Room."

I have fought and won my share of battles while meeting with God in my prayer chair. Glancing at it now, I see it looks even more lovely than it did the day I bought it. It's been a solid and sturdy chair through the years. I thank God for how he meets our needs, even in unlikely places like a Goodwill store. You may not have to shop in a thrift store, but the chair you donate could become someone's answer to prayer! Never underestimate what God can do for you and through you!

ACTION STEP: Find a comfortable chair or a cozy corner to journal your thoughts and prayers. Is there something you need but haven't asked God to supply?

From an Old Journal Entry:

I am sitting in my blue wingback chair at 10:40 p.m. The lights in the living room are dim, and the Christmas tree's white lights illuminate reflections on the wrapped gifts beneath it and the cross at the top. I just finished reading Psalms and Proverbs, Judges, and Ruth. I am now in the book of Samuel, but my eyes are so tired they keep tearing. The house is so warm and quiet. All I hear is the faint ticking of the old clock behind me. As I look around my house, I feel so blessed. God brought us here in His great wisdom, and I'm thankful He did. As I look at the nativity scene beside my chair, it almost seems to come to life. I feel like I am there, and my love for Jesus is being renewed moment by moment.

CAMELOT

> "By wisdom, a house is built, and through understanding, it is established; for through knowledge, its rooms are filled with rare and beautiful treasures." (Prov. 24:3–4 KJV)

When my daughter, Hannah, was almost three, word came that Tom's fourteen-year career as an engineer for General Dynamics was ending. Homes at the time were challenging to sell, and jobs in aerospace were next to impossible to find.

After being childless for almost fourteen years, the last thing I wanted to do was work outside the home to pay for daycare. It had always been my dream to be a stay-at-home mom. Wasn't I supposed to be the mom raising *homegrown kids*? I wondered if this might be an opportunity to start my own daycare.

The economy had taken a terrible turn for the worse; it didn't seem fair at the time. Yet God's Word assured me He had a plan for my life. Not to harm me but to bless me. He knew long before I did how my dreams would all fall into or out of place. So often, we can be tempted to give up when sacrifices are required. I was prayerfully determined to trust God every step of the way.

After praying to be Spirit-filled, my ears were opened to the supernatural, and so was my heart. It was becoming clear that God was leading the way for me to return home. A storm had been brewing in my life, and all I could do was look toward heaven and ask, "Now what, God? Please give me strength."

I had prayed so faithfully for more than a year for my aunty, who needed in-home care. I had been praying relentlessly that Tom would be hired by another company in San Diego before his layoff at General Dynamics. These were both significant needs. Amid it all, I feared I would have to place my daughter in daycare, and like so many of our neighbors, we could lose our home. Once again, I was looking to God as my provider.

Considering the distance between Visalia and San Diego, we had been helping Aunty financially because there wasn't much else we could do to help her. Her home was a six-hour drive from our home in San Diego. Tom was working six days a week. I worked part time at the National Network of Youth Ministries, and our daughter was only two. My dream of being a stay-at-home mom appeared impossible. Scripture tells us nothing is impossible for God, so I asked God for yet another miracle.

In less than twenty-four hours we had received our first miracle. I had just gotten off work and was walking to the mailbox when our next-door neighbor asked how things were going. He wanted to know if Tom had any leads on a new job. Which he did not. Asking what we would do next, I told him we needed to contact a realtor and try to sell our house. Bobby asked what we wanted for it. I told him what we "needed," and without blinking an eye, he told me he and Carol would buy it. They would buy it at the price we needed, and his realtor friend would do the paperwork.

The following morning Tom and I sat at our next-door neighbor's kitchen table, signing papers to sell them our home. The next miracle was an eighteen-day escrow confirming God was in control, and the "winds of change" were blowing us back to Visalia.

Just like that, we were moving, and life was about to change drastically! We were leaving the beautiful suburb of Rancho Bernardo, where sports cars, minivans, and SUVs were in every driveway. Leaving behind all the amenities we had taken for granted during those years we had enjoyed living in Sabre Springs. We were moving into Aunty's thirty-two-year-old house in the same neighborhood I had grown up in. Two prayers were being answered with one move! We would be there to help Aunty at the end of her life. And we could pay off the remainder of her mortgage, allowing me to be a stay-at-home mom without a monthly payment!

Taking on a fixer-upper was challenging with a three-year-old. But at the same time, it was one of the most rewarding tasks I had taken on up to that point. I remember someone in San Diego asking if the home we were moving to would have a nice view. I told them our "new" house didn't have air conditioning, doors on the closets, a dishwasher, or a garage, and no view unless you count the 100-year-old oak trees in the yard as a view. The house had a carport and a ten-year-old swamp cooler, but other than that, it was old and reeked of animals, rodents, and tobacco.

When I was growing up on Atkins Drive, the area was considered a genuinely nice housing tract for young families. Our neighborhood was considered a county island surrounded by beautiful vineyards, cotton fields, sweet corn, fruit ranches, and walnut groves. How things had changed on the north side of town. The neighborhood fruit stand was bulldozed, and a Food 4 Less grocery store swallowed up the land that once had been a flourishing vineyard. The surrounding farmland had been replaced with low-income houses, apartments, and small condominiums. We would soon see that God had a plan and a purpose for us living in that neighborhood beyond what we saw on the surface. We were missionaries placed there by God. Our faith was stretched, and our joy made full.

The house needed repairs, and the yards were desolate with weeds two feet tall. A thirty-two-year-old, broken-down redwood fence hid debris and junk piles that had accumulated for many years at the back of the property since the house had been built. Old tires, wheels, and carpeting. Chunks of cement, glass bottles, rusted-out lawn chairs, old garden hoses, and aluminum cans. But something in me saw beyond the neglect. Our tiny home and yard had potential! Maybe even a secret garden where kids would run, play with pets, and plant seeds of every kind . . . Vintage fruit-packing boxes from beneath that trash heap would make great nesting boxes for chickens.

With a lot of hard work and quiet times, my vision started taking shape. One by one, new pets came to live at *Our House*. Baby kittens hiding in the woodpile, baby chicks in the coop, and carnival goldfish thriving in a pond we made from an old wash tub found in the rubble. Puppies chased the kittens, and we had birds of every kind. One Thanksgiving Day, we were ecstatic to discover that our two rabbits had become ten! Is there anything cuter than baby bunnies?

Everything seemed to flourish at "Our House," especially the children's imaginations. What started as an extremely stressful set of circumstances became our place of simplicity. Many of my dreams came true, and souls were saved.

As a small child, I had promised Aunty that I would take care of her when "I got big and she got little." God allowed me to keep that promise to her. She enjoyed four months with us fixing up her old house, making it *Our House*. I remember her sitting in the living room after I had called for an ambulance. She looked at me and said, "I never thought I'd live in such a beautiful house." Prayers were answered, and God had provided. Oh, how I wish Aunty could have seen what God did when we were faithful with the little we had.

One Mother's Day, Tom and the neighbor kids made a great tree swing that hung from a large branch in one of our oak trees. Tom and all the kids each took turns pushing me as high as they could. It was the best tree swing ever! Eventually, we built a small barn with a loft and windows, which I used for storage, and the kids used for a clubhouse. The old metal shed was transformed into a charming potting shed and coop for the chickens to roost at night. Friends lovingly referred to *Our House* as "Camelot" (a place associated with glittering romance and optimism).

Tomatoes grew abundantly in the rich, fertile soil of the San Joaquin Valley. Sweet hens laid fresh, brown eggs daily, and there was always enough to share with the neighbors. Tom was a wonderful fix-it guy who enjoyed turning *Our House* into my dream of a country cottage. It was as cute as anything I had seen in magazines. We were resourceful and learned the art of re-purposing everything imaginable. Through prayer and petition, God provided everything we needed. Tom's fix-it skills and spray paint, coupled with my creativity, we created a cozy home we loved for eleven years. When I remarried after losing Tom, a teacher I worked with bought *Our House* with the big backyard and has raised her little family there.

As I write, it sounds like a fairytale. But we worked hard and developed spiritual muscles that strengthened us during our times of adversity. I'm not sure why bad things happen, but I believe God has a purpose in everything He permits to come into our lives.

There have been times when I couldn't resist crying out, "God, why is this happening to me?" Maybe that's where you are right now. Being honest with God is okay. He calls us his children, and He takes delight in us.

Sometimes when we pray, God answers immediately, and sometimes He waits until the time is right according to His timeline. Not all things are good, but God can engineer our circumstances so that good triumphs over what the enemy meant for evil.

Isaiah teaches us that God's ways and thoughts are higher than ours (Isa. 55:9). We see the momentary struggles, but God sees the beautifully completed bigger picture.

> "And I will bring the blind by a way that they knew not; I will lead them in paths that they have not known. I will make darkness light before them and crooked things straight. These things will I do unto them, and not forsake them." (Isa. 42:16 KJV)

ACTION STEP: What are you facing today? Is there something you need to cry out to God about? He's listening.

CHRISTMAS WOOD

"And my God shall supply all your needs according to His riches in glory by Christ Jesus." (Phil. 4:19 KJV)

*E*ach year as summer began to fade in the San Joaquin Valley, I cheerfully anticipated the cooler days of fall. It was my favorite time of year, but I started to see it differently on our non-existent budget. With the Christmas holiday around the corner, there was never a budget for Christmas gift-giving, and I was becoming weary of finding creative ways to give meaningful gifts to people I loved. The bills due in December didn't change because it was Christmas. Our financial sacrifice at that time was Christian education for our daughter. I was beginning to dread thoughts of Christmas gift-giving.

My dad was always a generous man, especially during the Christmas season. I grew up in a home where my parents were the original Black Friday shoppers. Our Christmas tree was up the day after Thanksgiving, and my parents were out shopping with our wish lists in hand.

My mom always had a festive cookie table with our favorite Christmas cookies, Grandma's old-fashioned sugared walnuts, and fudge. Dad would come home every other day with Christmas sweets and treats to add to the goodie table. Gifts soon began piling up around the Christmas tree and eventually around the perimeter of our family room. The fireplace kept burning, and we watched classic old movies like *Miracle on 34th Street* and *It's a Wonderful Life*.

During my daughter's childhood, materialism was at an all-time high. With my childhood memories of extravagant gifts, I felt pressure to make Christmas just as memorable for my daughter. But the one thing my family hadn't provided was the true meaning of Christmas. The holidays, when I was growing up, had been devoid of spiritual truths.

I didn't have Christmas money, but I was determined to ensure that the baby Jesus had a birthday party in our house, where needy kids were blessed and the real meaning of Christmas was celebrated. God honored that and continued to bless us with the things money couldn't buy. Memories we still cherish to this day.

Kneeling one morning at the foot of my bed, I began pouring my heart out to God. I told him I was weary of all the materialistic gift-giving expectations at Christmas. I apologized to Him for making my prayer about me when Christmas is about His Son. I ended my prayer by letting God know that if He wanted me to give gifts to people that Christmas, He would have to supply them because I had no way of doing it. I dried my tears and got in the car. The Spirit led me once again to the local Goodwill store where something extraordinary was about to take place.

As I walked in, I was first greeted by the familiar smell of old books, clothing, and shoes. To my knowledge, my mom had never stepped foot into a thrift store until that day. God had an interesting way of blessing me in unique and unusual ways while shopping at thrift stores.

It was a cold, gray November day, my mom was killing time in the Goodwill, waiting for my sister Denise to join her for lunch. Denise was driving thirty miles of foggy country backroads from Porterville to Visalia when she passed a place with a sign on the road: "Free Wood." She had quickly jotted down the address to give me, not knowing I would be joining her and Mom for lunch thirty minutes later.

She told me about the place advertising free wood, and I was very interested. My tiny house had no fireplace, but we had one in the garden. We loved sipping hot chocolate and coffee by a crackling fire during the cold winters. The thought of free firewood was worth a country drive, especially on such a cold and foggy day.

After a quick lunch with Mom, Denise and I were on a mission to get a trunk of free wood. We slowly pulled up to the old building that had rusty cars in front but didn't see firewood which was clearly advertised on the side of the road. A guy came out to greet us and assured us the wood was free, but we would have to load it ourselves. He looked at my Nissan Altima and then toward a large stack of wood pallets. "Is that the free firewood?" I asked, glancing at the small trunk of my car. We had driven eighteen miles for what we thought was firewood. I couldn't hide my disappointment.

Behind the guy, on the cinderblock building, was a small sign with two words that caught my attention: LOVE INC. I asked him what it stood for, and he said, "Love in the Name of Christ." Then he asked if I was a teacher. I was ... but ... I worked part time at a Christian School, teaching junior high and high school elective classes. As it turned out, LOVE INC. was a store of complimentary teacher supplies. To him, my being there was a divine appointment. He was excited for me to tour the building and learn about their ministry to teachers in Tulare County.

Once inside, it was like a mini-Costco. Industrial shopping carts, metal shelving, and concrete floors. The guy handed a clipboard to me, explaining that everything had an item number, and a quantity number of how many items I could get. Was I dreaming? Billy Graham's newest book was the first thing I saw, and at once, it made me think of my dad. What a perfect Christmas gift it would be for him. He loved Billy Graham. Then I saw the [1]Emily Barnes book *If Teacups Could Talk*, which I knew my friends would love.

When I left LOVE INC, my car's backseat and trunk were full! Along with Christmas gifts for everyone on my list, I left with rolls of brightly colored Christmas paper, Scotch tape, bows, ribbons, and gift cards. I had gifts for everybody I knew—including my pastors, teacher friends, neighbors, students, and family. It was pretty amazing.

As I was about to leave with my carload of gifts, the guy reminded me that it was the end of November and that I could shop once a month—which meant I could return a week later and fill up my car again! God provided most miraculously!

It became clear to me that God loves a cheerful giver. Right then and there, I knew God had heard my heart as I had knelt in prayer that morning at the foot of my bed. What had seemed a bust in my search for free wood turned out to be a double blessing in disguise. Once again, God's economy is quite different from ours. I wonder how many needs go unmet simply because we do not ask.

> "... but those who seek the LORD lack
> no good thing ..." (Ps. 34:10 NIV)

ACTION STEP: Finding God's provision in unlikely places. What are you seeking His help with today? Are you willing to go wherever the Spirit leads you?

FAULTY FUEL INJECTORS

"I cried unto the LORD with my voice; with my voice unto the LORD did I make my supplication . . ." (Matt. 9:16 KJV)

The fuel injectors in our ten-year-old car were leaking fuel, with strong vapors, beneath the hood, which could cause a fire at any given time. My husband, Tom, was so discouraged. Knowing we didn't have a budget for such a significant car repair, he asked me to pray about it. It could cost a thousand dollars or more to be fixed, he said.

God's Word says we can pray about anything, so why should we hesitate to pray when financial resources are limited? I had been doing the Henry Blackaby *Experiencing God* Bible Study and understood the difference between a necessity and a luxury. Immediately I took this need before God, hoping I wasn't wearying Him with yet another need.

Tom's unemployment had run out, and so had our savings. With his degree in engineering and fourteen years of experience, we had assumed he would have no problem securing employment after our move back to Visalia. He had interviews but would be told he had too much experience, or needed more specific experience.

Tom often dreamed of starting his own business, and this seemed like a door God might be opening. He had been using Tom's gifts and talents to help people in need during his season of unemployment. He did it as a ministry and loved helping people. Unfortunately, if he wanted to start a business, it would require capital, which we didn't have. We had a car that needed new fuel injectors, and it was too small to use even if it were in proper running order. It was a small two-seater sports car with a hatchback. There was no room for toolboxes, a ladder, or parts that might be required.

Not long after I had prayed to replace the fuel injectors, Tom was sorting through a stack of accumulated mail, separating junk mail from the bills due. He began opening a large envelope that he assumed to be a promo advertisement, but the look on his face told me that what he held in his hand was much more than advertising. When I questioned him about it, his reply was, *Experiencing God!* Slowly he began reading aloud the letter he held in his hand:

> "Dear Mr. Bunting,
>
> *In 1984, when your 300ZX was built, it was made with the finest materials known to man. However, new fuel additives have caused a disintegration of the fuel injectors. If you take this letter to your nearest Nissan dealership, we will replace your fuel injectors free of charge."*

Unbeknownst to us, Tom's Service and Repair was about to be launched. What had started as a ministry of Tom's—helping people with handyman jobs—appeared to be opening a new door to his longtime dream of starting a business.

At that same time, my sister was going through a divorce and asked Tom to help her sell her husband's small Mazda pickup. It wasn't an old truck, but it had been used as a farm truck and was extremely dirty. She offered to pay Tom to go through it mechanically, ensuring it was sound and detailing both the interior and exterior. She also asked him to oversee selling it so she didn't have to deal with strangers answering the newspaper ads.

While at Bible study, I shared our prayer request to find a buyer for Tom's two-seater sports car. That evening, we received a message on our answering machine. My Bible study leader could not believe it when she heard me saying we had a car to sell. She and her husband had prayed just the night before for a good used car they could buy for their son while he attended law school in Los Angeles. They didn't want to buy a brand-new car but didn't want to buy something used that could be unreliable, costing more money for repairs.

The need to sell our car was met within twenty-four hours of praying for a buyer. The following day my friend and her husband came with cash in hand and insisted on paying more than we had asked.

My dad, knowing Tom needed a truck if he were going to start his own business and my sister needed to sell one, offered Tom $2,000 to continue doing his and Mom's weekly pool service, and maintenance of their aging house and cars. Tom became the owner of the truck he had been meticulously detailing. Tom's Service and Repair was birthed.

Tom continued doing ministry projects for church and community members who lacked money for repairs. We did not become wealthy people through his business, but our needs were always met, and Tom was doing what he loved doing. Isn't that the way God works? His blessings always seem to touch more than one person at a time, as was surely the case in this situation.

One summer, Tom helped a couple of teachers who worked with me at the Christian school who had car repairs they couldn't afford. In return, we got something we could not afford: Summer tutoring and horseback riding for our daughter.

> "The LORD will guide you always; he will satisfy your needs in a sun-scorched land and will strengthen your frame." (Isa. 58:11 NIV)

ACTION STEP: Is there something that has been weighing you down? Something you've been praying for to no avail? Is it possible God is waiting for you to surrender your will to Him? Maybe it's time to wave your "white flag" and surrender it to Jesus. What might that look like for you?

UNUSUAL OPPORTUNITY FOR HOSPITALITY

"Offer hospitality to one another without grumbling." (1 Peter 4:9 NIV)

An unusual opportunity for hospitality presented itself one morning during my "quiet time" of all times. There was a knock at my door, and at first glance through the peephole, I was hesitant to open the door. I saw a bedraggled man in dirty clothes with a look of desperation on his face. I recognized him as a man known in the neighborhood as Screwy Louie. He had lived in our community most of his adult life, plagued by addictions that led to crimes that landed him in jail more times than he could count.

I opened my door and listened as he spun stories of why he needed to "borrow" money. Some neighbors gave him money just to get rid of him. Others threatened him with calling the police. They knew that any money given to him would most likely be used to support his habits.

I had nothing extra in those days, but I opened my wallet and emptied its contents into his weathered hands. All I had was three dollars and some spare change. I assured him repayment wasn't necessary and that God always meets our needs. I explained that I didn't have money to give in the future, but I always had food to share if he got hungry.

At that time, we had been living below the poverty level, yet God never failed to meet our needs. One evening, not long after Screwy Louie knocked at my door to "borrow" money, another knock came at my door. Screwy Louie stood there again on the other side of my locked screen door. His back and shoulders slumped, and he was gripping his stomach with both hands. His twisted face reflected both hunger and neglect. I could tell he had not had a decent meal or a bath in quite some time, and I don't think he owned a shirt or a pair of shoes. Remembering what I had told him when he had asked me for money, he asked if I could spare a bologna sandwich.

I think my spontaneous excitement at his request startled him. "Boy, did you pick the right time to come!" I excitedly explained to him how a coworker had blessed me with a twenty-pound frozen turkey she had received at Christmas and hadn't cooked. She was cleaning out her freezer and gave it to me. I told him I had a beautifully browned turkey on the table, homemade mashed potatoes, gravy, green bean casserole, and my favorite cranberry Jell-O salad topped with cream cheese! He practically drooled when I asked if he preferred white or dark meat. I asked him to sit on the porch and give me a couple of minutes to assemble a plate for him. Then I loaded a large, sturdy paper plate with a little bit of everything I had made and loaded up a wooden tray for him to carry everything home.

At first, I hesitated to send him home with my wooden serving tray. It had been a special gift from Tom shortly after we were married. But there was no way he could juggle it all without a tray. The Holy Spirit quickly reminded me that people are more important than things; it was just a wooden tray.

I will never forget the look in his bloodshot eyes as I opened the door to hand him "Thanksgiving in April." He slowly took the tray in both hands, looked at the feast before him, and began sobbing. Head down, shoulders shaking with each sob. When he looked up at me, tears were streaming down his face. With deep gut emotion, he said to me, "God loves you, Lady."

As hoped, my wooden tray was returned to my porch the following morning. It wouldn't be the only time my wooden tray with food would be handed to Screwy Louie through the screen door and promptly find its way back to me.

Today that wood tray is just a memory that reminds me of the ripple effect of generosity. Someone gave that turkey to a coworker, who blessed me with it, and I, in turn, blessed the hungry man who knocked at my door. He had hoped for a bologna sandwich and received a feast fit for a king. "Now all glory to God, who is able, through his mighty power at work within us, to accomplish infinitely more than we might ask or think." (Eph. 3:20 NLT)

My hospitality was indirectly affecting others in the neighborhood.

My parents were touched by watching Screwy Louie leave carrying meals home from my house, then leaving the tray on my porch the next day. My daughter would watch for him and excitedly helped me prepare his plates. Initially, my parents had discouraged me from extending hospitality to Screwy Louie because of his reputation. However, one evening my mom said, "If you don't have anything to give him, send him to my house, I always have plenty to share."

Something in my dad's heart was changing too. Billy Graham was scheduled to do a crusade in Fresno, about forty-five miles from Visalia. My dad said, "If I have to walk on my knees to get there, I will." He did get there, and that night he asked Jesus to forgive his sins and come inside his heart. Soon after, Dad became a chaplain for the police department, and the day he was sworn in, a small cross was pinned to the lapel of his uniform. I cried with joy and admiration at the transformation I was seeing in him. The man who had been lost was found. A man retired from a life in law enforcement was now a volunteer, extending the hand of mercy and grace to those in tragic situations.

Mom had started attending a small Pentecostal church, and one night, while I was soaking in a bubble bath, I heard her familiar knock-knock at my front door; then the bathroom door burst open, and my mom stood there grinning from ear to ear. She wanted to know if I would attend church with her the following Sunday to see her be baptized. I felt like her little girl again for a moment, though I was probably forty years old. Mom turned and left as quickly as she had arrived. I called out to my husband from the bathroom, "Tom, who was that woman?" From then on, she was a changed person, loving God and actively serving in her church.

God worked miracles in the eleven years I lived in that downtrodden housing tract off Houston and Ben Maddox. I've been asked if I ever experienced feelings of fear when neighbors like Screwy Louie came to my door. I felt cautious, but God had called me back to that neighborhood as a missionary. The fears I experienced were like those that most missionaries experience in foreign places. Especially where the neighboring people are hostile to Christianity. Not all my neighbors lived at the poverty level. But spiritually speaking, most were bankrupt.

One night we had a team of police officers surrounding our home. They were not quiet, and neither were their highly trained canines! After a stabbing at the neighborhood Jack in the Box restaurant, a gang member jumped our fence to hide in our backyard. We watched from our living room window as the man was apprehended and taken into custody.

On another occasion, a different neighbor, high on meth, tried to come through our front door. He was frantic and said someone was trying to kill him. My husband Tom told me to call 911, then went outside and waited for help to arrive while the guy hid in our shed.

Another unusual opportunity to extend hospitality was to a neighbor named Hope. God allowed me to minister to her on a winter night when the valley temps threatened to freeze citrus crops and burst uncovered water pipes. She showed up at my door in a thin nightgown and a pair of old socks knocking frantically at my door. She screamed to me to let her in—that her son was trying to kill her! I couldn't let her in the house with my young daughter getting ready for bed, but Hope's teeth were chattering from the cold.

Interestingly I had been doing laundry and just finished drying a load of blankets, so I sat her in the wicker rocker on my front porch, covered her with the warm blankets, and handed her a cup of steaming hot chamomile tea, hoping it would calm her. At the same time, I waited for a return call from the rescue mission. As a mission volunteer, I knew who to call, and a room was quickly reserved for Hope.

I had not formerly met her before that night, but she had run straight to my house. As she was warming up beneath the blankets, she asked me if I would pray for her. Kneeling beside her, I gently began praying, touching her head, then her shoulders, moving down to touch the top of her feet. She thanked me for praying, and I kept her company until her ride got there. She cried, and I patted her hands through the blanket. Then with a sweet, loving voice, Hope said, "Honey, I don't even know your name, but I knew you were a Christian because of the aura around your head." Her son, who just happened to be Screwy Louie, got another trip to jail that night, and Hope went to the mission for a hot shower and a safe, warm bed to sleep in.

It was another opportunity to share what little I had with the least of these. When God calls us to something, He says, "Fear not, for I am with you."

> "In the same way, let your light shine before others, that they may see your good deeds and glorify your Father in heaven. (Matt. 5:1 NIV)

ACTION STEP: How might you let your light shine before others? Can you remember a time in your life when someone's generosity allowed you to see Jesus in their eyes?

SMALL AS A MUSTARD SEED

"Or what woman, having ten silver coins, if she loses one coin, does not light a lamp and sweep the house and seek diligently until she finds it?" (Luke 15:8–10 ESV)

I'm sipping hot tea, enjoying a winter snow flurry outside my window, and I'm reminded of the winter I discovered an empty facet to my wedding ring. I hadn't noticed the diamond was missing until slipping my hand into the pocket of my cozy, fleece bathrobe before bed. That's when I felt my ring snag inside my pocket. How long had my diamond been missing? I began mentally retracing my steps throughout the day. I had spent the first half of the day doing laundry, cooking, and hand-washing dishes. The remainder of my day was spent planting flats of brightly colored pansies and English primrose, and tending to our menagerie.

My first thought was to check my gardening gloves, but it was too dark in my unlighted garden. Remembering all I had done that day only reassured me of my doubts about finding something so small. I had cleaned the chicken pen, adding fresh straw bedding to each laying box. If I had lost the diamond in the chicken pen, it would have been gone in a flash! Chickens are drawn to anything shiny. I had fed them that day, added fresh water to their waterer, and raked every inch of their yard and the roosting barn.

Our old house on Atkins had been built before dishwashers were standard kitchen equipment, making it all the more likely my diamond had gone down the kitchen sink straight to the septic tank. I had done a lot of cooking that day, which also meant a lot of handwashing of dishes.

Tom being the "inventor" he was, strapped a flashlight to his head and crawled on hands and knees, searching carpet fibers throughout our house. I think watching the children's movie *Honey, I Shrunk the Kids*, starring Rick Moranis, may have inspired his search. If not for such sad circumstances, I would have laughed hysterically watching my husband with his face to the floor, magnifying glass in hand, searching for a tiny lost diamond.

My heart was broken, and I couldn't imagine not wearing my rings. After several days had passed, I decided to take an old earring made of cubic zirconia (synthetic diamond) to a jeweler and have it placed in my ring. It might not be authentic, but it belonged to my aunty and would allow me to continue wearing my rings and give me another story to tell.

I was retelling the sad story to a friend at Bible study, and she asked me, "Have you prayed to find it?" She had lost a piece of jewelry and found it shortly after praying. I had little faith that God cared about something as small as a mustard seed, but I took my friend's advice and prayed.

The Valley weather was cold and foggy that January—perfect weather for being cozy inside, watching afternoon movies with my daughter. Hannah was probably in kindergarten at the time and crawled under the puffy comforter on her bed to watch old Shirley Temple movies. I snuggled under my heated blanket and had trouble keeping my eyes open. As I was dozing off, Hannah said, "Mommy, I think I found your diamond!" I was thinking, *Probably one of her Barbie earrings.* With one eye half open, I held out my hand to her. As she placed it in my hand, I could hardly believe it. It was my diamond!

She had found it between the sheets in her bed after feeling what she thought was a grain of sand. It made perfect sense! Her bedding had been the last of many loads of laundry I had done the day when I noticed my diamond was missing. What were the chances? It could have been under the sheet or at the foot of the bed. She could have quickly just moved her leg or brushed the annoyance away. But something told her to look at it, pick it up, and show me. You might see this as coincidental, but I saw it as an answer to my half-hearted prayer to find that which was lost.

Immediately I jumped up to call the jewelry store. I hoped they hadn't already placed the dull imposter into my wedding ring. As it turned out, the jeweler had taken a few days of vacation, so they had not had a chance to do my ring. They were as amazed as I had been when I explained how we had found the diamond. Hannah and I jumped in the car and drove straight to the jewelry store, where they promptly appraised my diamond. I was told it was a Blue Diamond, and though small, it was a quality diamond worth much more than Tom had initially paid. Even though I had prayed with just a "mustard seed" of faith, God allowed me to find that which was lost.

Now that ring has been passed down to my daughter, a mom with her own daughters. The diamond she had found for me so many years earlier found its way back to her in the toe of her Christmas stocking that had been hung on the fireplace. That morning, Tyler Jewell slipped it on her finger and asked her to marry him. She said, "Yes!"

As impressive as it was to find a missing diamond, it wasn't the only one I would lose. Several years ago, I noticed one of my diamond earrings was missing. It had been a hectic day after Christmas, putting away decorations and dragging the dried-out, brittle pine tree to the trash. I could have lost my earring in any number of places that day. By the time I noticed it was missing, the same feeling came over me that I had experienced after losing the diamond in my ring. This time I began praying immediately, even though it too seemed hopeless. Could it be possible that history and faith might repeat themselves once again?

Before falling into bed that night, I grabbed a flashlight, looked around the bed, checked the closet, and retraced my steps in the bathroom. No luck. Then the Holy Spirit whispered, *Look under the bed.* While shining the flashlight beneath the bed, a bright sparkle caught my eye like a lighthouse on a dark night. There it was! Another diamond that had been lost was found.

I wonder if that's how God feels when His light shines on us. Once lost, now the light of Christ reflects His light which is in us. Never underestimate what God might do when you seek Him. Have you lost something precious? Have you prayed about it? God cares about even the most minor things in our lives. *"I tell you there is rejoicing in the presence of God over one sinner who repents." (Luke 15:8–10 NIV)*

ACTION STEP: Is there something you have lost? Have you prayed? Do you know someone who is lost and without direction? Why not pray that they will be found?

From an Old Journal Entry:

Prayer is the key that unlocks so many mysteries. Often it is the last thing we do. Why is that? Do we think God can't or won't hear or answer when we ask Him for his help? Scripture tells us that God rejoices when one of his sheep is found. We are the sheep, and He is the shepherd. We were lost, but now we are found. Prayer changes everything.

WINDS OF CHANGE

Chinese Proverb: "When the winds of change blow, some people build walls; others build windmills."

What I love about the changing of seasons is that they are predictable, and we look forward to the weather changes coming. We begin to anticipate the changes and start preparing for them in advance. Buying sweaters and jackets in the fall. Or shorts and sundresses in spring and summer. Our calendars and national holidays also help us know when to expect seasonal changes in advance. It's not so easy to predict or prepare in advance for life changes, which can come in different ways at any time. Perhaps an unexpected pregnancy. Or the sudden loss of a job. Maybe losing a loved one before their time. We don't always know what is around the corner. An excellent reason to . . . *be prepared in and out of season* . . . (2 Tim. 4:2 NIV).

A mysterious stirring that I can't explain was happening in my soul in 2002. A dark storm was brewing, and though I could not see it, I felt it in my spirit. Something inside me told me to draw nearer to God and hold on tight. My quiet times got longer and quieter, and I listened intently for God's still, small voice. Reading the Scriptures was becoming even more intentional and insightful.

Having just finished reading *The Prayer of Jabez* by Bruce Wilkinson, I was very aware that God is the source of my blessings, whether emotional, physical, spiritual, social, or financial. I was also aware of my need to pray, asking God to keep me from harm, pain, despair, and anguish, knowing only He could protect me.

It had been a small, easy book to read, perfectly fitting my lifestyle of simplicity. The author of that small book challenged me to make the simple Jabez prayer my daily prayer. By the end of thirty days, I noticed some significant changes happening in my life. But I had no idea how my "territory/influence" was about to increase beyond my wildest imagination. That simple prayer was becoming a treasured style of simplicity to my prayer life. God was using those times to build me up and strengthen me in the faith.

Dark clouds of doubt and fear were heading my way. The winds of change had come in quietly and then hit like a hurricane. It was a storm that threatened to destroy me and everything I held dear. Without the solid foundation of faith that Tom and I had built, I probably would not be here today, testifying to God's goodness and faithfulness through it all.

Suddenly, I found myself questioning the circumstances of my life. If God was blessing me, I certainly didn't feel it as I was sitting in the waiting room of the surgical center. Tom had had an endoscopic procedure, which revealed an exceptionally large tumor. There was nothing the doctor could say to give me hope. They gave my sweet husband six months to a year to live, encouraging him to get his house in order. We were in the eye of the storm. Through it all, Tom was my rock, and God was my protector.

About seven months after Tom's diagnosis, Hannah got home from school, and she ran to the bedroom where her dad was listening to his favorite Christian music. He had been lying on the bed pondering the doctor's latest update. Hannah had been so hopeful he would get a good report. Tom remained quiet, and she reminded him that God could still do a miracle. He looked at her and said, "Sweetie, Daddy is sick, and I'm not getting better." He told her to promise him that even though she didn't get the miracle she was praying for, she would never forget the miracles God had already done in her life and those He would continue to do.

What happened next was like a scene from a Hollywood tearjerker. Tom talked to Hannah with the gentleness and compassion of a good father. His eyes were tearing, but he had calm strength. He assured her that God was not asking anything of him that He would not ask of everyone someday; He was just asking it of him sooner than we had hoped.

The power of the Holy Spirit was with us, and Tom's words were about to give a prophetic glimpse into my and Hannah's near future: "Sweetie, where I'm going, I have no fears or worries. My only concerns here are for you and Momma. She is still young and has her life to live. If a nice man comes along and wants to love her and take care of you, I do not want you to say, 'Daddy wouldn't want that,' because all I want is to know that you guys are loved and taken care of. I promise you; she will be the most discerning woman."

I have never admired a man more than I did Tom Bunting at that moment! It spoke so much of his gentle Christlike character and faith. Though his body grew weaker as time passed, he was never stronger than in the heat of his battle to gain heaven.

Today I'm re-reading the prayer of Jabez in 1 Chronicles 4:10: "...*Oh, that you would bless me and enlarge my territory! Let your hand be with me and keep me from harm so I will be free from pain.*" This Scripture shows us that asking God to bless and protect us is okay. A blessing is much greater than a material possession. Spiritual blessings are what we find in good friendships. It's a peace that surpasses understanding and a belief that all things will work together for good (Rom. 8:28).

When Jabez said, "Let your hand be with me," he knew his own limitations and feeble nature. I did too! When I first talked to Kevin O'Connor, he asked me about my spiritual gifts. I told him, "I have no special gifts, talents, or abilities." He didn't believe it for a second. At that moment, everything in my life of simplicity was about to change. My territory was about to be increased!

Eighteen years ago, I married a man in full-time ministry. God most assuredly was about to increase my influence. Today, Kevin and I live in a quaint mountain community thirty-eight miles south of Big Bear, California. Yucaipa is a hidden gem in Southern California best known for its apple orchards, walking paths, and small-town charm. I love its four seasons with winter snow especially.

As my influence increased, so did the square footage of my home. I cannot guarantee that the size of your house will be enlarged, but I believe that God's hand is on you, and He will guide you on the right path for the journey set before you. Jabez's prayer honored God, and he had the right attitude when he prayed. God heard Jabez's prayer, and God granted what he asked.

"You will go out in joy and be led forth in peace; the mountains and hills will burst into song before you, and all the trees of the fields will clap their hands." (Isa. 55:12 NIV)

ACTION STEP: Evaluating what you know about God is essential to approaching Him with a proper attitude. Do you know that God alone is your source of blessings? Do you believe he knows how to answer appropriately to all your needs? If we pray for the wrong things and God says, "No," will you trust His will? Pray "Thy will be done," and you'll warm God's heart.

From an Old Journal Entry:

    Lord, I feel the winds of change blowing. Is that your Holy Spirit's way of preparing me for the changes I might face? It's strange. When I should be depressed, worried, and questioning Your love for me, something assures me that You have a plan and a purpose even for this. I trust you to work even this tragic situation together for good. Yes, for a good purpose. How? That's not my concern today. Today I will be obedient and trust You with Tom, Hannah, myself, and even the broken pastor You've given me a burden to pray for. If prayers are like seeds, something is growing in the garden of my heart . . .

A MIGHTY RUSHING WIND

"... And suddenly there came a sound from heaven as of a rushing mighty wind ..." (2 Sam. 22:2 KJV)

More back story: Tom Bunting was playing tennis at the College of The Sequoias, I was finishing my senior year of high school. Each day after school, Tom would pick me up at the tennis courts and take me out for lunch. It was a sweet relationship, and we enjoyed each other's friendship. Tom graduated from COS and was accepted to Cal Poly San Luis Obispo, which is a small coastal town midway between Los Angeles and San Francisco.

After a year apart, we knew it wasn't for us. In the Spring of 1978, Tom proposed to me with a small, solitaire diamond engagement ring at our favorite bench along the creek behind the Old Mission San Luis.

We knew that if we wanted a honeymoon, we would need to plan the wedding before the fall semester began. We chose the second week of September and were married at the Nazarene Church in Visalia, where I had worked during high school. We honeymooned in Hawaii, and Tom's classes began two days after he carried me over the threshold.

Tom and I loved shopping at local farmers' markets, health food stores, and the fresh seafood markets near us. Friends called us health food fanatics, so when Tom was diagnosed with pancreatic cancer in 2004, it was a complete shock to us and everyone who knew us! We both remained active and healthy throughout our twenty-six-year marriage. Tom was an avid tennis player and never weighed five pounds more than in high school.

After being told on Valentine's Day, 2004, that Tom's cancer was advanced, his doctor scheduled him for surgery at USC in Los Angeles. We were told this surgery would not save his life, but it would give us more time together as a family, which we were very grateful to have. It took a couple of months to recover after his surgery, but we kept a positive outlook and recognized each day as a gift.

After Bible Study one morning, a friend asked if Tom and I would stop by her husband's office that afternoon. Being an attorney, he wanted to help us with legal matters we hadn't considered up to this point. It wasn't a long meeting, and after signing the necessary papers, they handed us a manila envelope to open. In it were keys to their spacious mountain home in beautiful Lake Tahoe. Our twenty-sixth wedding anniversary was just a couple weeks away, and they wanted to bless us. The idea of spending an entire week in Lake Tahoe sounded amazing to both of us! Neither of us had ever been there. As we left their office, they assured us everything would be ready when we arrived. What an incredibly generous and thoughtful gift.

We drove to Lake Tahoe after what had been a long workday for me. The illness was progressing, and Tom wasn't feeling very well, but knowing this would be our last anniversary together, we wouldn't complain, even during the five-and-a-half-hour drive. We finally arrived around midnight; it was too dark to see or appreciate our surroundings. Lights were left on at the cabin, making for a warm and inviting welcome. Besides the soft lights shining through the windows, the only other thing we could see was what seemed to be a million stars overhead! Did you know that Philippians 2:15 compares believers to lights shining in the world? Psalm 147:4 says God counts the number of stars and calls them each by name.

Once inside, we did an exciting, quick tour of the home. The beds were so inviting. With their oversized mattresses, fluffy down comforters, luxurious pillows, amazing sheets, and plush bath towels, we knew it would be a great week.

The following morning, we awoke to the deepest blue skies, bright sunshine, fresh mountain air, and the reality of spending five precious days together off the beaten path. There was a quiet hush amid the towering pine trees—it was a place to be still. The spacious cabin seemed even more significant during the day, with windows from floor to ceiling. Five beautiful bedrooms and three bathrooms on three distinct levels. It seemed enormous compared to our nine-hundred-square-foot house with one bathroom. When we opened the refrigerator, it was fully stocked. Fresh local produce, seasonal fresh fruits, and cuts of lean, flavorful meats for grilling on the large deck.

We would take our coffee to the deck in the mornings and were in awe of the beauty surrounding us. Our daughter was thirteen at the time, and we had taken her out of school to spend that special week with us. We enjoyed watching her carefree moments feeding peanuts to inquisitive squirrels and curious scrub jays with their bright blue feathers, white wing bars, and jaunty crests of feathers.

Journal entry that day: *"Lord, surely you are with us in this place. We feel your hand is upon us and sense your Holy presence."*

One thing I had asked to do while in Tahoe was to have a couple of hours all to myself. I chose Sunday morning at daybreak, eager to spend that time with God. Grabbing my Bible, prayer journal, and a large mug of coffee, I walked deep into the forest, searching for a place to "have church."

It didn't take long for me to find the perfect spot. A large, fallen pine tree would be my "pew for one." Looking up through the tops of the pine trees, I watched as light filtered through the branches like morning light coming through stained-glass windows. Fragrant pine needles carpeted the ground beneath my feet. The aromatic fragrance of the early morning forest was almost intoxicating.

Noticing a tree stump a few feet away, I saw rays of warm sunlight radiating from above which would be the altar where I knelt and prayed, *"God, I want to hear your voice. I want to feel your touch. I want to see your face."* The only words to explain what I experienced after that prayer would be "frightening" and "exhilarating."

I began to hear a rapidly moving roar of wind approaching me from a great distance away! It reminded me of the sound I once heard in the Sequoias during an avalanche. It was a mighty rushing wind, and it was coming towards me with tremendous speed! The wind around me became fierce, and debris fell from the trees around me in seconds. There was no place to shelter, and I stood there frozen with my head down. Then the roaring wind left me as quickly as it had come upon me. Complete and utter silence. I most definitely heard God's voice and felt His touch. I did not see His face, but I know He saw mine! In Acts 2:2, the Scripture tells us, *"Suddenly a sound like the blowing of a violent wind came from heaven and filled the whole house where they were sitting. (NIV).* My little church in the forest experienced Pentecost!

Several weeks after that experience, I encountered God's voice again. Only this time, it was as soft and gentle as a dove, almost a whisper as I was kneeling at the foot of my bed. God had my undivided attention, and what He said to me that morning, I now know, was most definitely a prophetic glimpse into my future.

"For I know the plans I have for you declares the LORD, plans prosper you and not to harm you, plans to give you hope and a future." (Jer. 29:11 NIV) Never underestimate what God can and will do when you are fully surrendered to Him. He's waiting for you. Ask Him to reveal Himself to you today, and then wait, watch, and listen! What He has done for me, He is willing to do for you too. Ask, and it shall be given.

Do you have a quiet place outdoors, away from life's busyness, where you can seek God's presence? Before I had a backyard, I sought out parks and walking trails. Some of my most memorable early morning walks with God occurred in the small beach town of Cayucos, California, where Tom's parents lived. When visiting them, I would get up early before anyone else in the house was awake and walk on the beach talking with God. It was always special!

ACTION STEP:

From an Old Journal Entry:

    Thank you, God, for this life you've given me. Thank you for seeing me through various trials and difficulties, especially during those years before I knew you as my friend, Father, and protector. Lord, thank you for my health and strength of body and that I can enjoy bike rides along the river with my daughter, work with kids, and keep my house and yard nice. Lord, help me not to take this life for granted. Help me to be content even when I have needs. Help me keep things in proper perspective, not forgetting who my authentic self is. Help me raise my daughter well. Thank you for a good marriage and a happy home. I want to serve you simply all the days of my life. Amen.

MY WALK TO REMEMBER

"But Ruth said, 'Do not urge me to leave you or turn back from following you; for where you go, I will go, and where you lodge, I will lodge. Your people shall be my people, and your god, my God.'" (Ruth 1:16 NAS)

The St. John's River in Visalia was one of my favorite places for bike riding and water play during hot summer months which the San Joaquin Valley is known for. St. John's River is a large, controlled release of water downstream from the Terminus Dam when the snow melts in the mountains. Along the river, benches are provided for resting and taking in the view of the Sierras. There is less water flow in the winter, but the backdrop of the snowy mountains is majestic to look at on a clear day.

Though I've been on this trail countless times, one day stands out above all the rest, never to be forgotten. I call it my walk to remember. It was Thanksgiving Day 2004. Tom's cancer had progressed, adversely affecting everything, especially his appetite and digestive system.

I suggested a short walk along the river, and he agreed it would be a nice breath of fresh air. St. John's was only about ten blocks from where we lived, making it a short five-minute drive. I parked as close to the riverbank as possible, knowing how weak and frail Tom had gotten. Arm in arm, we strolled. How many times had we taken this walk for granted? We walked the familiar path, saying very little. We treasured another walk together, knowing it would most likely be the last time we would walk that familiar path.

The sky was clear, and the temperature was a comfortable sixty-three degrees. The trees and bushes were showing off their vibrant November colors, and for whatever reason, we were the only ones at the river that afternoon. Standing near the large spillway, I shared something with Tom that I had recently experienced during my time with God. "Tom,

I don't sit around and think about remarrying, but several weeks ago, I had a strange thing happen. I was crying out to God to heal you. I said, 'God, if you do not heal Tom, what will happen to Hannah and me? Who will help her with math?' Then I heard a voice behind me speak. It was a comforting voice, but it was not necessarily reassuring. It sounded like a male whisper. I opened my eyes, glanced over my shoulder, and said, 'God, is that you?' He repeated the question, word for word: 'Mindy, if I had a broken pastor who lost his wife and church, could you come alongside and encourage him?' After He repeated the question, I responded, 'Yes, God, but what does that mean?'"

I looked up into Tom's kind, expressive eyes at that moment and asked him if he thought I could be a pastor's wife. He told me he thought I would make a wonderful pastor's wife. We hugged each other tight and let our tears flow.

In my heart and mind, I could not imagine why God would say something so perplexing to me at such a troubling time. People have asked if it might have been my wish instead of the voice of God. Why, at that time, would I ask God to send me someone broken? Someone whose livelihood was something I felt entirely unequipped for. With so much brokenness around me, the last thing I would have wished for was more brokenness.

When I shared this with a few of my closest friends, they listened but had no idea how to respond. I have had people since that time ask me why I would share something like that with a spouse dealing with his own mortality. That is just the kind of relationship Tom and I had. We were honest and open with each other. We were stepping into the unknown together.

I was about to become a widow and a single mom at forty-eight. I had to take over the responsibility for our finances for the first time, and I had no idea what I would do. Spreading the bills out on the kitchen table, I prayed, "Father, I cannot pay these bills. Your Word says you will be the husband of the widow and the father of the fatherless. I am spreading these bills before you, my Jehovah Jireh. Thank you for your provision."

Jehovah Jireh is the name for God which means "The Lord Will

Provide." It appears three times in the Old Testament and reflects the Lord's covenant promises to provide for His people. I had already gone to the County Services office, hoping for temporary help, but I was turned down. As I left the Social Services office that day, a couple of other people were waiting their turn to apply for assistance. I sat down for a moment, looking at their faces, and I prayed, "Lord, if these people qualify and I don't, please have mercy on them."

Well-meaning friends suggested I put my house and cars in my parents' name to make me eligible for food stamps. When I told Tom what had happened and what friends were saying, he looked at me with his drawn face and said, "Mindy, that wouldn't be very honoring to God." From that very moment on, groceries supernaturally began coming to our door. Checks came from people we knew, as well as people we did not know. The bills got paid, including high medical bills and deductibles. We did what was right in God's eyes, and He was honored, and in turn, we were blessed.

What you have will be enough for today. Put God's Word to the test and watch to see how blessings come in the most unexpected ways. God sees, He hears, and He cares! Thank Him for His involvement in your life today and trust Him with your tomorrows.

> "He who is faithful in a very little thing is faithful also in much, and he who is unrighteous in a very little thing is unrighteous also in much." (Luke 16:10 NASB)

ACTION STEP:

From an Old Journal Entry:

January 24, 2005

The Lord came and took Tom home. Tonight, a new chapter begins in my life. Now it is just Hannah and me. Pastor Bob Somerville said that many people call death the afterlife, but this life is actually the beforelife, and once we die, we will begin to experience real life. That's an incredible way to look at it. Lord God, you know me. There is nothing I can tell you that comes as a surprise to you. I know you will bless Hannah and me in ways I can't imagine. Use me, Lord. You see the end from the beginning. Thank you, God, for the work you've been doing in my daughter's life. I love her, Lord. I believe you have good plans for her future. I'm unsure why you have allowed us to endure this heavy trial. Keep us focused on you, Lord, and I know we'll be OK. Thank you, Dear Lord, for loving us. Amen.

YOU WANT TO READ MY JOURNALS?

"You yourselves are our letter, written on our hearts, known and read by everyone. You show that you are a letter from Christ, the result of our ministry, written not with ink but with the Spirit of the living God, not on tablets of stone but on tablets of human hearts." (2 Cor. 3:2–3 NIV)

Sitting on the floor, peering through the glass doors of my antique bookcase, I'm momentarily paralyzed by the magnitude of life's ordinary yet extraordinary moments. What started as a handwritten journal to leave a legacy to the next generation has become an enormous collection of my life's ordinary moments experiencing the extraordinary God.

Each book represents the different seasons of my Christian faith. Stories that otherwise would have been forgotten now beckon me backward in time. As I open the first door, my eyes go straight to the dark, smoky-colored journal from December 2004. "Pick me," it seems to say. Hesitantly, I reached for it. Holding it gently, I remember that time when I needed God most. Slowly turning one page and then another, I see my familiar penmanship from late-night entries of a time as dark as the cover of my journal. *"Hospice says Tom 'turned a corner.' Time is short. Every moment precious."*

I'm unaware of how much time has passed, sitting cross-legged beside the antique bookcase. Part of me wants to skip over my December 23, 2004 journal entry. But something is drawing me to revisit this day from so long ago. Slowly I begin to read . . .

I remember telling a friend, "I feel the winds of change blowing." Was that the Holy Spirit's way of preparing me in advance for the changes I now face? It's so strange . . . at a time in my life when I should be depressed, worried, and questioning God's love for me, something assures me that God has a plan and a purpose for my life. Will He work even this tragic situation together for good? Yes, I know He will. If prayers are like seeds, something is growing in the garden of my heart! It's two days before Christmas, and I'm wondering how the rest of my life might play out. Will I ever write the book inside me? Will I one day experience new adventures and romance? Will I ever bless others out of prosperity, or is poverty my lot in life? Will I possibly see old and new dreams come to pass? Build the new home I've dreamed of? Travel to new places I've never been. I remember the night Tom told me I have too much love to give not to be married. It made me cry. Is it possible that one day, as Tom said, my heart might go on?

As for today, it is my privilege to meet my husband's needs, in sickness or health, until death us do part. I must leave dreams of better days here, where they are kept safe as I face today's brutal realities. I love my husband, but God asks me to love Him more, trust Him more, and serve Him more. I will continue to praise God in this storm. Lord, let my obedience be a witness to the faith I have found in you.

Turning one page and then another, I begin reading my entry from Christmas Eve 2004:

My cup runneth over. My life is in God's hands. It's Christmas Eve, and we have had steady visitors all day. Three men from Tom's tennis club came to our door and said, "We are the three wise men. We come bearing gifts." They had brought us a check for one thousand dollars and said they would return to prune trees for me after Christmas. My principal also came bearing gifts. One thousand dollars in cash and another thousand dollars in gift cards! Most assuredly, our needs are being met.

Christmas Morning 2004:

Hannah and I opened the front door to walk to Mom and Dad's for a quick Christmas breakfast. Upon opening our front door to step out, we were stunned at what awaited! Someone had come in the night and placed over sixty beautiful red poinsettias in the carport, creating a vibrant red and green path from our front door to the driveway. It took my breath away. An unbelievable sight at 6:30 a.m. on a cold, gray December morning. We never found out who it was that demonstrated such thoughtfulness late that Christmas Eve.

Skipping a few pages, I turn to the day of Tom's Celebration of Life, dated January 28, 2005:

Lightning lit the sky as we drove onto the church grounds. The rain pounded on the roof overhead, and thunder peels penetrated the large church's walls. A musician seated at the black, baby-grand piano sang "I Can Only Imagine" by Mercy Me. I hadn't noticed but was told that almost 500 people were in attendance.

That afternoon as people began leaving, I gathered up the memories I had displayed on a table representing Tom's life: his Varsity letter jacket, tennis racquets, sports trophies, and remote-controlled cars. It was a quiet drive home for Hannah and me, but the dark sky was beginning to show breaks in the clouds. We rounded the corner to our street, greeted by the most beautiful double rainbow that seemed to end right in our backyard! We had made it through the storm that day, literally. God did not promise we would not experience storms, but He has promised He will be with us during them.

The memories of that year were becoming more manageable. The healing process had begun, and life was moving forward. Quietly I close my journal and, holding it to my heart, I thanked God for how He had seen me through those days and brought me to where I am today. In the book of Genesis God sealed His promise with a rainbow in the sky in the midst of devastation, symbolizing His gracious promise.

God had used a timely, brilliant, double rainbow to remind me of His presence and power during the storm. Then He began to unfold a new chapter of "rainbows and revelations" in my life. Things I had prayed about were coming to pass. The things I had been journaling for years were about to reveal the continued plan God had ordained for my life.

The best was yet to come. When I first *bumped* into Kevin O'Connor, we both knew something supernatural was happening, but it was hard to believe. After we had met several times in person, a friend of mine invited me to bring Kevin to their home for dinner. Kevin arrived and rang their doorbell. My friend's husband opened the door and told Kevin, "Let's take a walk." My friend and I giggled like schoolgirls as we watched the two men in what seemed to be a serious conversation. Pastor Brian had asked Kevin if he knew about "the broken pastor" I had journaled about.

They came back in, and we had a very nice dinner. Before leaving, Kevin asked me if he could read a few of my journals. Surprised at his asking, I said, "You want to read my journals?" He followed me home, and I handed him the ones he seemed most interested in reading.

With my journals in hand, Kevin made the 100-mile drive back to Merced in record time and began reading my most intimate journal entries from the last year of Tom's life. Before turning out the light late that night, Kevin says he fell asleep with one of my journals on his chest. The following morning, I woke to find an email from Kevin. He said he had fallen in love with me while reading my journals.

I have found journaling to be an art of processing life, death, and everything in between. Is there something you need to process? Something you haven't wanted to say out loud but need to work through? Why not write it here and ask God to guide you as you face whatever lies ahead? It's quite possible the best is yet to come.

> "Now unto him that is able to do exceedingly abundantly above all that we ask or think, according to the power that worketh in us . . ." (Eph. 3:20 KJV)

ACTION STEP:

HOPELESSLY ROMANTIC

"Many waters cannot quench love, nor floods drown it . . ." (Song of Solomon 8:7 NKJV)

Before Kevin and I had actually met face to face, we got to know each other very well through email writing and phone calls lasting late into the night. It didn't take long to realize we were a "match made in heaven." Not everyone saw it that way; many were quick to judge. From their perspective, I had not grieved long enough, and Kevin had not been divorced long enough. (*We didn't disagree with that.*)

What Kevin and I saw as a divine meeting, others saw as something I should run from. They had difficulty understanding that God had been preparing me for months, possibly years before I would know who Kevin O'Connor was. God had asked me six months before I heard Kevin's name if I could encourage a broken pastor. That didn't mean much to them. It had been quite perplexing to me at the time, but it set into motion many conversations I would have with God as to why He would consider me for such a task, even before my husband's death. One thing I have learned is that God's ways aren't our ways. He does not expect us to understand everything, but He does ask us to trust Him and walk in obedience to Him and His Word.

After Kevin and I *mysteriously* bumped into each other on a dating website offering a free twenty-four-hour trial, Kevin had allowed the computer to choose his username—"Extr3mely Handsome"—which almost caused me to skip right over his reply to my icebreaker question, especially since there wasn't a profile photo attached! On the other hand, I had chosen something more spiritually inclined— "Sincerely His"—in which only a Christian man would see and discern the hidden meaning. After sharing a few lighthearted instant messages, I clicked out of the app, leaving him hanging at the other end. I had some help from my thirteen-year-old daughter and other things to do.

That evening I knelt to pray after a very interesting day. Something in me was saying, *Look that guy up.* I returned to my computer after Hannah was in bed, but I couldn't find "Extr3mely Handsome." (He unsubscribed after my daughter blocked him). He had deleted the free temporary profile, feeling dejected by my abrupt disconnect. He had no way of knowing then that Hannah was the one who had blocked him after lecturing me on all the dangers of talking with strangers online.

In the brief moments Kevin and I had chatted, I created a paper trail of what he had told me, just in case my daughter was right, and I ended up in the trunk of a car! After finding no trace of a guy called "Extr3mely Handsome," I went to the handwritten notes on the notepad beside my computer. He had given me his church's website address and name. Either he was legit, or he was some guy impersonating a large church pastor a hundred miles from where I was living.

The following morning, I sent a simple, straightforward text saying, "My name is Mindy, and if you'd like to talk, this is my phone number." He called an hour later. It wasn't a long conversation, but I loved his voice. It was soft and kind, possibly cautious under the circumstances. He was about to go into a meeting and asked if he could call me after work.

We were two very different people meeting in an improbable way! After many hours of phone conversations, we planned to meet in person at a restaurant in Visalia. When one of my friend's husbands heard that I was planning to meet a guy I had met online for lunch, he said, "No, you aren't! Young lady. You are grounded!" I had survived Tom's year-long cancer battle and felt alive again. I wasn't going to let someone "ground me" at my age.

Kevin lived in Merced and pastored an independent church called Christian Life Center. We talked every night, and he would call every morning to pray for Hannah and me. I enjoyed our conversations and found his lifestyle much more demanding than my life of simplicity. He was also a man of greater sorrow than I had experienced. We were there for each other during a trying time in both our lives. I was learning how to be a single working mom. Kevin was learning how to be a single pastor. I had planned a funeral after my husband's death, and he was planning a "funeral" after the death of a marriage. We planned to meet in person that upcoming Friday.

Kevin ended up surprising me three days early—entirely unexpectedly! I saw him from the corner of my eye as he slowly walked toward my driveway. He was wearing black jeans and a crisp, collared shirt. My first reaction to seeing him in person was, "Oh my gosh!" He was handsome, and he brought me gifts!

The only photo we had seen of each other, up to this point, was no bigger than a postage stamp. So, we really didn't know what to expect before our first meeting. It was a quick introduction with a sidearm hug, and he assured me he would be returning Friday to take me to the restaurant of my choice.

In the gift bag was a small painting of a rainbow he had bought from a local artist at the retreat where he had been the keynote speaker in Washington. Beneath the painted rainbow was a small rock, on which the artist had painted a small ark and the words, "God keeps His promises." There was also a card, which he asked me to open later.

Cash fell out of the card when I opened it that evening, which caught me off guard. His office manager had told him that a family in Visalia had ordered several sets of his sermons on CD. He had said to Gwen, "I'll hand deliver them." The CDs I had ordered prompted his early unplanned visit to Visalia that afternoon. Inside the card, he had written: *Mindy, anytime you pay for something I would give you freely, you'll get back more than you paid.* (Prov. 11:24)

When he asked where I'd like to meet for lunch Friday, I chose to meet at the old train depot that had become a restaurant renowned for its fabulous food. The building had been restored to its original elegance and atmosphere from the days when it had been the Southern Pacific Railroad Depot, originally built in 1916. The Depot had been gorgeously restored with a mix of timeless elegance, European architecture, and stained-glass art pieces imported from Italian church ruins. Beautiful chandeliers were imported from Spain, and stunning, crystal glass windows had emerged from a century-old New Orleans hotel. There would be no shortage of ambiance.

My first visit to the old train depot was as a child while picking up a family member who had ridden the train from Texas to Visalia for Christmas. Many years later, after it had been converted to a restaurant, Tom and I held our wedding rehearsal dinner—and subsequent anniversaries—at The Depot. Besides its rich architectural history, there was no shortage of personal history for me there.

Skipping ahead twenty-six years later, a new memory was about to be made at The Depot. Kevin opened the large, wooden double door and we stepped into the dim lighting, which instantly gave us that soft-touch photography look. Servers wearing gold and black tuxedos were attentive and helpful. Each table adorned with white linen table coverings and the warmth of real candlelight. At my recommendation, Kevin ordered my favorite entree on the menu: *calamari with lemon butter sauce*. We savored every bite. After a delightful lunch, dessert and coffee were served. Is anything better than crème brûlée?

Kevin reached his hands across the table, holding mine, and he said, "Mindy, you have to marry me!" When I laughed aloud, he leaned forward and gently began to bang his head on the table. I laughed again at his exaggerated gesture, but he had my undivided attention. We just stared into each other's eyes for a moment, knowing Kevin had just taken things to a new level in our friendship. It was time for pastoral counseling.

The day we sat in Pastor Carl's office, I knew I was being interviewed for more than marriage. I was being interviewed for the possibility of a "ministry" marriage. As our meeting ended, Pastor Carl announced with a smile: "I'll do the wedding." As lovely as it would have been for everyone who knew us to have been as happy about us as Pastor Carl was, and as happy as we were, our deepest desire was to please God. The one thing we both knew at that stage of life was what we didn't want. Our personalities seemed like fire and gasoline, and knowing God's plan for intimacy after marriage, we knew it wouldn't be a long courtship. When sharing this with others, we received a fair amount of criticism. But we knew that on judgment day, it wouldn't be friends or family we would stand before. We would be answering to God.

Kevin officially proposed to me on a Sunday morning in his office between church services. He had invited a few special friends and family to be there. He got down on bended knee to slip a diamond ring on my finger, asking me if I would become his wife and partner in ministry.

The summer of 2005 became a blur of meeting new people, shopping for a nontraditional dress, and planning an intimate, outdoor wedding. The friends who initially had invited Kevin to their home for dinner lived on a private lake, and it seemed the perfect spot for a simple yet romantic wedding venue! The wooden dock would become the aisle I would walk toward my smiling groom.

As I had envisioned, Kevin was standing on the dock in his black tailored suit, freshly ironed, white dress shirt, and wearing a champagne-colored tie. He waited for the boat to arrive, bringing his bride as the sun began descending in the west. From where I stood on the front of the quiet patio boat, I could hear the famous Celine Dion song "My Heart Will Go On" played by a violinist beneath the white-lighted gazebo. I felt like a princess in champagne lace, carrying a white rose and two wedding bands. Almost everything was as I had imagined the night to be.

One thing I had not anticipated was the emotional moment I would have while reciting the traditional wedding vows. When Pastor Carl said, "In sickness and health, unto death us do part," I got choked up and started to cry. I leaned into Kevin's chest and whispered, "I can't say it." His soft response was: "I'll wait." Everyone waited and felt my emotion, knowing I had already done that once. After a few moments, I regained my composure and completed the saying of my covenant vows: "I, Mindy, take you Kevin . . ."

Kevin had booked the Loews Coronado Bay Resort on Coronado Island for our first week together as husband and wife. Waking up that first morning in San Diego, my husband walked to the mini-fridge and returned to bed with something behind his back. Reaching out with two spoons, he smiled and said, "Pick your weapon." In his other hand was a large crème brûlée dessert topped with fresh fruit and berries that he had thoughtfully ordered from the hotel bakery the night before. Since that breakfast in bed eighteen years ago, Pastor Kevin continues to be my hopelessly romantic knight in shining armor.

"In a large house, there are articles not only of gold and silver, but also of wood and clay; some are for special purposes and some for common use. Those who cleanse themselves from the latter will be instruments for special purposes, made holy, useful to the Master and prepared to do any good work." (2 Tim. 2:20–21 NIV)

ACTION STEP:

THE BLENDING OF A FAMILY

"The LORD is near to the brokenhearted and saves the crushed in spirit." (Ps. 34:18 ESV)

The blending of two families can be challenging, they said. Who said this? Friends who had remarried after divorce and pastors who had counseled blended families.

When Kevin and I married, he had such a tender heart for my daughter, Hannah. At that time, she was only fourteen and still dealing with the recent loss of her dad. That in itself was a lot to overcome. Add to that a remarriage for Mom, moving, changing schools, and becoming a PK (pastor's kid) within the same year meant many changes and challenges. Kevin and I agreed we would navigate those rough waters together, trusting God every step of the way.

God's Word was our guidebook. We looked at what the Scriptures had to say about remarriage after a woman is widowed (1 Cor. 7:8–9; 1 Tim. 5:14). Not only does the Bible not speak against remarriage after a spouse dies, but in some cases, it actually encourages it. During biblical times (2 Kings 4:1–7), remarriage was the primary way for a widow to regain protection and provision for her and her children. Remarriage after the death of a spouse is permissible by God.

Many well-meaning friends pointed out that Kevin was not a widower, but the sad truth was that his twenty-seven-year marriage had died. Truthful, painful, and unavoidable by the time he learned there was no path back to the wife of his youth. Some ask, did ministry life take a toll on their relationship? No, sin did. Does God hate divorce? Yes, but divorce isn't less forgivable than any other sin. We tend to focus on the greater sins in a marriage, like adultery. Still, we neglect to see the more minor sins leading to hardened hearts and despair that compound, causing distance and eventually leading to the death of a marriage.

In my wildest dreams, I never thought *divorce* would touch my life. "Christians don't get divorced. Especially pastors!" It was not just friends saying this. It was me too. The word *divorce* had been my first obstacle to overcome in meeting the "broken pastor," but now he had a name, a face, and a bleeding heart.

I reminded myself that God hadn't called me to *marry* a broken pastor. He had called me to encourage him. The spiritual backstory is always important in a Christian's life. At least seven months had passed since God had spoken to me regarding a broken pastor. Seven months of praying for and journaling about him before I knew his name. Only a few of my friends were privileged to know that backstory.

One morning, a male coworker pulled me aside and told me he thought my relationship with Kevin was moving too quickly. He suggested postponing the marriage for my daughter's sake. Softly I replied, "I don't believe God will bring something to my life that will destroy my daughter's life." It's been eighteen years, and I can honestly say it was more rewarding to please God than it would have been being a people pleaser.

Kevin and I knew what we didn't want in a marriage. A blended family wasn't a dealbreaker for us. We had fallen in love and knew that if we were to please God, we would need to move to marriage as soon as possible. God's Word showed us clearly that "to marry is better than burning with passion" (1 Cor. 7:9 ISV).

Naturally, from the start, my teenage daughter disliked Kevin stepping into our world. She would ignore him like he was not even in the room. When Kevin tried to converse with her, she suddenly had terrible hearing. I told her she didn't have to like him, but she had to be as respectful towards him as any stranger she met on the street, at school, or in church. Kevin assured me this was a typical teenage reaction, and he was emotionally strong enough to handle her pain and anger. He also reminded me that Hannah had few outlets for her anger and frustration. He chose to love her unconditionally, and I chose to love his sons similarly. As maturing adults, it then became their responsibility to make the same choices toward us.

At the time, a professional counselor we talked to told us about the different stages of blending a family. Kids don't have much say in their parent's decision to remarry after death or divorce. But they have a great deal of power in breaking up the relationship. Most stepparents have or will experience this to some degree. It's not just teens who can get hostile and reject their parent's new spouse. Even adult children wrestle with painful feelings like hostility and disloyalty, especially around the holidays. Regarding the blended family, my husband has always said: extend grace. Expect nothing. Appreciate everything.

If there is anything I've learned, it's to have realistic expectations. We knew not to expect enthusiastic teenagers or young adults. What we did expect was their respectfulness. Inviting them into your life is essential, but respecting their choice to decline, especially when they are adults, is equally important. This sometimes challenges our Christian ethics and sharpens our ability to love unconditionally. Something Kevin did so well.

Each night before Kevin would come to bed, he'd say, "Goodnight, Hannah." But she had "hearing issues" and never responded. She could hear him; she just chose not to. Many nights this happened, and she would not even turn her head to acknowledge him. Every morning he did the same thing before she left for school. "Have a great day, Hannah; I'll be praying for you." But he was the invisible man. No reply.

Kevin came home one night from a particularly long board meeting. It had been such a long day for him. He ambled up the stairs into our room and quietly closed the double French doors behind him. He had just slipped into bed when there was a knock at the door, and we heard a small voice say, "Goodnight."

Kevin cried, and we thanked God for this small, blended-family breakthrough. Every night after that, when Kevin said, "Goodnight, Hannah," she would say the same in return. It didn't take long in the grand scheme of things. She knew he was her protector and her provider. Not just mine. I asked him one night why he tried so hard when he received so little in return. He looked at me and said, "The best way to show a woman that you love her is to love her daughter." What a great example he has shown us of what the love of Christ looks like.

Our sin is what hung Jesus on that Calvary Cross. He was rejected, ignored, and laughed at. Hated, questioned, and insulted. What did Jesus do in return? He prayed, "Father, forgive them, for they know not what they do" (Luke 23:34).

Counselors say it takes about seven years for a newly blended family to adjust. Kevin says that the spiritual nutrients of a woman who regularly meets with an extraordinary God are more important than years spent. How can you show love unconditionally to the people in your life? Is there an area that needs forgiveness? Can you be the one to forgive and extend grace?

> "Steadfast love and faithfulness meet; righteousness and peace kiss each other. Faithfulness springs from the ground, and righteousness look down from the sky." (Ps. 85:10–11 ESV)

ACTION STEP:

DRAGONFLY AND A PRAYER

"Because he loves me," says the LORD, "I will rescue him; I will protect him, for he acknowledges my name." (Ps. 91:14 ASV)

*I*f you have not heard of Lake Placid, Florida, I hadn't either. It's a small lake in Highlands County, Florida, where Kevin and I were scheduled to attend a three-day conference at a waterfront resort area. It looked like the perfect place for a little getaway and what seemed to be an informative conference.

Lake Placid Camp and Conference Center is eighty-five miles south of Orlando. They offer various comfortable, modern lodging facilities, including deluxe villas, cozy cabins, dormitories, and historic mansions—each with unique charm and style. The website showed pictures of a white sand beach lined with tiki torches for relaxing, romantic evening strolls.

They listed fun activities and amenities: kayaking, fishing, and comfortable Adirondack chairs with umbrellas on the beach. It seemed like the perfect place for mixing church business with pleasure. We had anticipated our trip to Florida for months and finally had airline tickets in hand. That October, when we landed in Florida, we were greeted with hot temperatures and high humidity. It was a long travel day from the West Coast to the East Coast, and we were looking forward to checking into our room and catching a quick nap before dinner and the conference's opening.

We arrived and found our way to where our room was located. We could tell we were not in the high-rent district of the Lake Placid Camp and Conference Center. The room was not as inviting as we imagined our beach bungalow to be, but I was glad to see a small table next to the window air conditioner. I envisioned myself writing while my husband attended the three-day conference for pastors.

When we returned from dinner and meetings that evening,

swarms of gigantic blind mosquitos had invaded our room! The beds were small, but there were two of them, which was our first clue this would not be the most romantic place we had ever stayed. When I turned the light on in our tiny bathroom, our toothbrushes looked like black lollipops! That is when we discovered that ants in Florida love toothpaste! Armies of ants continued to come out of the woodwork. Kevin started fighting the ants with a can of Right Guard while I took on the mosquitoes. With one flip-flop in both hands, I jumped from one squeaky bed to the next, killing mosquitos on the ceiling and walls. There were too many to count!

Years of Florida humidity had caused our modular "motel room" to smell of mildew, which I knew couldn't be good for us. Each time we flushed the toilet, we had to reach into the tank to put the chain back on the float. We consoled ourselves that it was only three nights, and the air conditioner seemed to be working well.

On our first morning, the chef served us a fabulous breakfast. After the morning worship service, my husband went to the conference room, and I returned to our tiny room, excited to start the book I'd been saying I would write for fifteen years. I didn't realize then that one of the stories I would one day write about took place while we were there.

Long story short, the laptop I'd been given didn't work. After a couple of hours, I just gave up on it. Why waste an afternoon in a stuffy room reeking of mildew? I'd write the old-fashioned way with paper and ink. What was I thinking sitting in that moldy motel room when I had a beautiful lake and grounds to enjoy? With my Bible, journal, and notepad, I set out for a quiet place where distractions would be minimal. It was hot and humid, but the sky was gorgeous! In the distance, I could see a large wooden cross with a picnic table nearby which looked like the perfect place to spend quiet time with God.

It was a longer walk to the cross than it looked. Once at the picnic table, I glanced around the table for any possible ant hills. All seemed clear, so I sat down to soak in the sounds of nature and gaze at the beauty of the marsh reeds and cattails. Opening my Bible, I began reading, but my eyes were so heavy. I hadn't slept well the night before, knowing mosquitos and ants had complete access to our little bungalow. I lay my face down on my open Bible and began praying. The insects and birds were creating a chorus of sound that surrounded me. Crickets? Cicadas? Frogs? Birds? It was amazing.

After a few moments of resting my eyes, I sensed God say, "Open your eyes and look at your surroundings." Was it God? Or was the devil trying to distract me from my time with God? Again, I sensed an urgency to open my eyes and look up at my surroundings. A tiny black dragonfly was hovering like a miniature drone two inches from my face! It dropped to the picnic bench beside me when I looked at it. To my shock, that spindly dragonfly was taking on a giant spider! The body of the enormous spider dwarfed the tiny dragonfly. Without his bravery, I would have been oblivious to the danger an inch from my bare leg!

The dragonfly was clearly the aggressor in this dual. I cringed, not wanting to see this spindly dragonfly become the spider's lunch! The dragonfly stood its ground, and there was very little space between him and the fangs of that bulky spider, five times his size. If I had kept my head down, refusing to listen to the still, small voice speaking, the spider could have inflicted pain on me. I slowly stood up and away from the picnic table. After stepping away from the bench, I began doing the Jitterbug dance, ensuring nothing else was crawling on my back. I couldn't get out of there quick enough! On my walk back to the room, I described the spider to one of the groundskeepers, who told me it was most likely venomous, and many were out there!

God sent a little dragonfly to save me from a potentially venomous spider! He also sent His Son to save all who would call upon His name and ask for forgiveness of sins. If you haven't done that, maybe this story will help draw your attention to that still, small voice you sense speaking to you. You've got nothing to lose and everything to gain.

ACTION STEP: Can you think of a time when you sensed God speaking to you?

CRACKING THE CODE

"Consider what I say, and the Lord give thee understanding in all things . . ." (2 Tim. 2:7 KJV)

Walking into an antique store for me is like stepping back in time. Immediately I'm transported from this hectic life in the twenty-first century to a less hurried, uncomplicated era. After an enjoyable morning strolling through antique boutiques on Main Street Visalia, I made the mistake of commenting wistfully to my grandmother about the "good old" days. She set me straight very quickly.

Antique stores have allowed me to experience all the nostalgia and none of the responsibility. Pocket watches, weathered leather Bibles, and field glasses one might imagine having belonged to someone's great-grandfather. Seeing a colorful patchwork quilt faded through the years, I imagine a tired prairie mom tucking her children beneath on cold winter nights. What treasures might a young bride have stored in the wooden chest still with the aroma of fresh-cut cedar? I know because these sentimental things have been handed down to me by my maternal grandparents, and I will one day pass them down to my grandchildren. The legacy continues.

One of my favorite antiques is a blue cast-iron safe that belonged to my first husband's grandpa. Tom and I had been married twenty-six years, and I had never thought to ask him what the combination for the lock might be. The day Tom stepped into heaven he carried the combination with him leaving me to wonder about its treasured contents.

After I remarried, different people tried cracking the code. A retired military man in our church had been a safecracker. He was reasonably confident he could open it. He spent most of a day attempting to crack the code and gave up, saying we would have to allow someone to break it open if we wanted to know what was in it. I placed it back on the shelf beside Tom's tennis trophies, college diploma, and an old tennis racket.

A few weeks later, the conversation came up once again. Kevin's friend, Pat Whyte, from the East Coast, was visiting and wanted to look at it. With his skills in logic and numbers, Pat was determined, but he, too, gave up and could not crack the code. I took the safe from him, sat it on my lap, and prayed: "God, if you can walk and talk with Tom, would you ask him to help me open the safe?"

I spun the combination several times and listened for the tumbler clicks. I had no idea what I was doing, but the little door swung open within about thirty seconds. Kevin and his friend thought I was kidding. I held it up for them to see and said, "It was God! He helped me!" The contents inside? Exactly what I suspected: it was stuffed with love letters I sent Tom in 1977 while he was away at college.

I began to read those love letters aloud to Kevin and Pat. Another moment I cherish as God supernaturally and instantly answered a prayer.

Never underestimate the unlimited creativity and resources of your Heavenly Father. Why not ask Him now, and see what He will do? What do you need help with? A hard heart that's been closed to the things of God? A mind that can't perceive the love and forgiveness of an all-knowing God? Ask, believe, receive, in Jesus' name. Amen.

ACTION STEP:

WILL YOU BUILD A WALL OR A WINDMILL?

"The wind blows wherever it pleases. You hear its sound, but you cannot tell where it comes from or where it is going. So, it is with everyone born of the Spirit." (John 3:8 NIV)

An ancient Chinese proverb says, "When the wind blows, some people build walls while others build windmills." Walls are typically built to keep people in or out. Windmills, however, create power and energy, generating electricity, pumping water, and powering cargo ships. China's emperors built the Great Wall of China to protect their territory. Oftentimes when we experience some kind of trauma, we can be inclined to "build walls" to protect ourselves psychologically. The problem with walls is that they can close us off and create loneliness and superficiality.

How I came to become the wife of a man in full-time ministry at forty-eight is nothing short of miraculous! I haven't always been a pastor's wife. But when I felt the winds of change begin to blow, I leaned in and harnessed the power of the one who created the wind! It didn't come by building walls to hide behind. Though, at times, a wall may have felt safer than it did when leaning into the wind.

The winds of change seemed to come gently and mysteriously, like the gradual change from one season to the next. When the intensity picked up, I held tightly to God's hand. My future was uncertain, and those winds of change began preparing my heart for the saddest season in my life. We saw the ominous signs. The storm of a lifetime was heading straight toward us. There was nothing we could do to stop it. We did what most people do when the National Weather Service gives a storm advisory. We sheltered in place. Kept our eyes on the road in front of us. Called out to God to redirect the winds from our path. Instead of diverting the storm, He offered us His strength which carried us through it.

Tom and I would read Philippians 4:6 "... in every situation with prayer and petition with thanksgiving, tell your requests to God. Do not be anxious about anything. And the peace that surpasses all understanding will guard your hearts and minds in Christ Jesus."

All we could do at that time was to call on the power of the one who calms the raging sea. The same power that raised Jesus from the grave lives in us! Those are lyrics from one of my favorite worship songs, by Jeremy Camp, titled "Same Power." God's Spirit had come upon the disciples gathered on the Day of Pentecost, and "there came from heaven a sound" like a mighty rushing wind (Acts 2:2). Imagine for a moment you and I are in a quaint coffee shop or small cafe. Maybe a rustic garden or charming bookstore. Or perhaps we just met in the lobby of a hotel or possibly even a hospital waiting room. These are just a few places where I have re-told my stories to so many.

Much like the patchwork quilts my grandma used to make, the making of this pastor's wife is similar. Instead of fabric squares like Grandma used, God used life's situations, biblical truths, hardships, and faithfulness to bring me to this place. Steppingstones of experience, maturation, broken dreams, and new dreams brought me to where I am today. I was willing to take risks, make sacrifices, and walk in obedience to what God called me to. In return, I have grown and done things I didn't know I could do.

Jeremiah 29:13 says, "You will seek me and find me when you seek me with all your heart." I love that promise. It doesn't say we *might be heard* when we pray. It says we will be heard. Can you feel the gentle stirring of God's Spirit? The Spirit is the very breath of God, the wind in our sails that lifts us from the doldrums and gives us direction and power to do His will. Let's start knocking down the walls of negativity, doubt, fear, and unhealthy behaviors and build a windmill to harness the power of the One who sends the winds!

"The LORD is slow to anger, and great in power and will not at all acquit the wicked: the LORD hath his way in the whirlwind and in the storm, and the clouds are the dust of his feet." (Nah. 1:3 KJV)

ACTION STEP:

BEAUTY FOR ASHES

"He has saved us and called us to a holy life—not because of anything we have done but because of his own purpose and grace. This grace was given us in Christ Jesus before the beginning of time . . . (2 Tim. 1:9 NIV)

My husband once used an illustration in one of his sermons that I've never forgotten. On the big screen, he showed a photo of a bowl that had been broken. There is a Japanese art where instead of discarding broken vessels, they are repaired by filling in the breaks with a gold adhesive, adding greater value to what was broken. They take the broken cup, bowl, or vase and make them beautiful, not perfect. The word for "gold mending" in Japan is *Kintsugi* which literally means "gold mending," emphasizing the beauty and utility of breaks and imperfections.

My husband's illustration that day was about the Kintsugi, but he went on to share what the Bible says about something similar that happened in biblical times. Dishonest merchants would use melted wax to hide defects, like cracks in their pottery, to sell it at a higher price. By contrast, honest merchants would hang a sign over their pottery that said *sine cera* (without wax), letting their customers know their merchandise was genuine.

The Scriptures tell us we are like clay jars in which treasure is stored. The treasure inside comes from the real power of God within us (2 Cor. 4:7–9). Yes, this clay jar can be broken and flawed. But it gets refined when going through fiery trials. God takes each of us with our flaws and makes us into something beautiful and increases our value within the Kingdom of God.

Just as the gold lacquer gives the broken vessel uniqueness and value, the Holy Spirit does the same in us. Sometimes our brokenness comes from natural aging, accidents, or failures. Living in this fallen world, sometimes our brokenness comes deliberately from the hand of someone close to us. Someone who should have been our protector, but they were careless in handling us.

Sins one has committed against us, or sins we have engaged in, may have brought brokenness and destroyed innocence and trust. For the person with Christ inside their heart, He brings healing and forgiveness. God takes our flaws, insecurities, and failures and strengthens us.

Before I would meet Kevin or even know his name, God asked me if I could encourage a broken pastor. At the time, I had no idea what a "broken pastor" looked like, but if he had lost his wife and church, I was familiar with the brokenness death brings to families.

Through conversations with Kevin, I learned what his counselor had called "the death of a marriage." I did not know a man could cry so much! I remember my phone ringing one morning at 2 a.m. Knowing it was Kevin, I quickly answered. After praying for him, he asked me how it was that I could be such an encourager to him, as it hadn't been that long since Tom had passed away. I said to him, "Your pain is much greater than mine. I got to do 'until death do us part.'" He asked me, "Do you have another 'until death do us part in you?'" I said, "I do." The past eighteen years with Kevin O'Connor have been the fastest years of my life!

People wondered how it was that we could both move on so quickly. Through counseling and soul searching, Kevin saw that his divorce hadn't happened in a vacuum. God had started filling in the areas that had been broken. When asked if the ministry had placed too great of a burden on their marriage, Kevin answered, "No ... Sin is what placed the greatest burden on my marriage." Sin comes in many disguises. Like the dishonest merchants using wax to cover defective pottery, sin waxes hearts cold. Though we are Christians, we can still choose to harden our hearts and reject God's truth. It's so important to keep our hearts close to God and His commandments. Harboring anger, hatred, and unforgiveness is a heart issue. Matthew 24:12 tells us: "Because iniquity will abound, the love of many will grow cold."

God is a repairer, and He is preparing us for eternity. A place where we receive a brand-new body! No wax will be needed to cover or hide our flaws! You are not just an earthen vessel. You are God's work of art, becoming more valuable every day. You carry with you the treasure of God's gift inside.

> *ACTION STEPS:* Are there things you've been waxing over in your marriage or walk with God? Have you had a cold heart toward someone you love? God wants to create within you a clean heart and renew you with a right spirit. He wants to help remove deception, anger, and unforgiveness, restoring you in areas that have been broken.
>
> Counseling Services and Referrals are available through Focus on The Family's Counseling Department. Visit: FocusOnTheFamily.com/CounselingNetwork

FACE TIME GOD?

"The LORD spoke to you face to face at the mountain from the midst of the fire..." (Deut. 5:4 NASB)

*I*think everyone today is familiar with FaceTime. It can be easily used on a cellphone with a forward-facing camera. Technically speaking, FaceTime works by setting up a connection between two supported electronic devices. Initially, the FaceTime application only allowed a one-on-one video chat—only two people could talk simultaneously. I'm told video conferencing today can enable us to simultaneously participate in a video call with up to thirty-two people!

But did you know you can *Face Time* God? It's very "user-friendly," and there's no limit on how many people can simultaneously participate! You don't need a cellphone or any other device to have Face Time with God. There are no hidden fees or Wi-Fi connections necessary! When I said this to my granddaughter, Paisley, her eyes got big, and she said, "God has a phone?" My answer: "No, God has something better!"

Having a relationship with God is just like a relationship you have with anyone else in your life who you want to spend time with. The difference between FaceTime on a device and *Face Time* with God is about His Power that makes the connection possible! When you *Face Time* with God, you'll never hear the word *unavailable* or get routed to a voicemail. Prayer is the direct connection between us and God. Talking to God through prayer can take place anywhere! But there are times when we need to move from prayer to petition. I call that *Face Time* with God!

What's the difference between prayer and petition? Biblically the difference is in the usage or intensity of the request. Think of a petition like a 911 call requesting God's immediate help with something. I activate Face Time with God by opening my Bible on the floor, lying face down on the open pages, and crying out to Him, begging for immediate help—whether it's something I personally need or someone

I love desperately needs. We've never lost connection, and He has been faithful in my times of great distress.

My next step is like "writing a 911 report" of the incident. This is where you journal about your "911 call" and Face Time with God. Developing a routine quiet time is crucial if you want a meaningful connection to God. God speaks to us through His written Word, His Holy Spirit, prayer, and sometimes through circumstances. Reading the Bible, praying, and resting in God's presence will rejuvenate you spiritually. If you want to experience a more intimate relationship with God, you'll need a quiet place to spend time with Him. For a busy mom, it might be while the kids are napping or before you go to bed after they have been tucked in.

If your house or apartment is small, be creative. A lighted closet, the car, the front porch, or the balcony are all great places! I've used all of these! During a trying time with a house full of people, I discovered something by accident that has become a great place to go when I need to unplug. After buying a sofa sleeper for our small home-office, we upgraded to a higher-quality mattress. Not realizing La-Z-Boy would deliver both mattresses, I needed to quickly stash the extra mattress while our company was here. I stood it up in the master bedroom closet, and as soon as I turned my back, it dropped to the floor.

I had been so busy preparing for our company that I saw an opportunity and dropped on the mattress to catch my breath. I put sheets and a soft blanket on it and called it my decompression chamber. It was so comfortable and tranquil! I'm not the only person who has loved "the closet." Without asking permission, I won't volunteer the names of the people who have slept in that closet. The mattress has since been upgraded to a Tempur-Pedic, and it's the coziest and quietest room in the house!

I knew a lady that turned an outdoor shed into a "prayer closet." It had an antique bed with pretty, floral bedding, a reading chair with a lamp, and treasured antiques.

Another busy mom I knew lived in a single-wide mobile home and found it impossible to find a quiet place to do her morning devotions. Her husband and kids knew not to bother her when she was in the bathroom. She got very creative and remodeled the bathroom! Fresh paint, wallpaper, matching towels, rugs, flowers, and a small candle transformed a practical space into a palatial spot to meet with God. You've got this!

> "And they will tell it to the inhabitants of this land: for they have heard that thou LORD art among this people, that thou LORD art seen face to face, and that thy cloud standeth over them, and that thou goest before them, by day time in a pillar of a cloud, and in a pillar of fire by night." (Num. 14:14 KJV)

ACTION STEP: Find a chair, desk, table, or another place to journal your thoughts and prayers. You can always talk to God, but He would love to Face Time with you today!

ADDENDUM

I'd love to hear from you . . . If you have discovered a new joy in journaling, I'd love to hear how God is working in your life through journaling your prayers. The following story was written by one of our international students who lived with us while attending high school in Redlands, California. She recently started journaling in hopes of drawing closer to God. When Quyen shared her story with me not too long ago, I asked her permission to share it. It comes from her heart, and she hopes it might help someone else grow and discover journaling to a new level of spiritual intimacy with God.

I want to hear from you if you have been inspired to begin journaling your prayers! Maybe one of your stories will be part of the addendum in my next book! Email me your story: Mkoconnor910@gmail.com.

Sincerely His,
Mindy

GOD A QUIET COMPANY

*S*ubmitted by Quyen Huynh. She was one of our many international students studying in America, helping make me a mother to many.

> "And surely I am with you always, to the very end of the age."
> (Matt. 28:20 NIV)

March 2023, written in Quyen's Journal:

Growing up, I often envied others' happy lives. As a child, I was admired for growing up in the most beautiful house in the city. (Ho Chi Minh City, Vietnam). While playing piano on the balcony, I often caught the attention of neighborhood kids, who would look up at me with admiration. At age six, I tried to switch roles with the maid girl around my age, tempting her with my princess bedroom and beautiful toys in exchange for her mother's daily noodle cooking. However, the child was unsatisfied with my offer; she couldn't understand why I wanted to swap lives with someone living in poorer conditions than myself. It begs the question, didn't God say, "Happy are the people whose God is Yahweh"? (Ps. 144:15 NRSV).

I found myself lost in the woods at night during a high school camping trip. As I trekked back to the cabin, I told myself that I would no longer need anyone if I could navigate this darkness and bitter cold. For thirty minutes, I held on to the hope that someone would find me with their light and wrap me in a warm embrace, telling me everything would be OK. But no one came, and I faced my fears alone.

It wasn't until I later read the Bible that I realized Deuteronomy 31:6, "Be strong and courageous. Do not be afraid or terrified because of them, For the Lord, your God, goes with you; He will never leave or forsake you." Looking back, I realize He was with me from above during that dark and scary time. Though the camping area was known to have bears that night, I was not attacked. Could it be the Holy Spirit was guiding me along the way? Though no one could locate me, I found solace in seeking Him. With God's help I found my way back to camp. More importantly I got saved and baptized by my American host dad. With this in mind, I am reminded that heaven will not be a place of cold and darkness. When I was lost the Father looked for me and I found His love.

I once couldn't find a reason to live and prayed for guidance. Now at age twenty-one, I contributed to opening a 6,000-square-foot homeless center in a faraway city where I had just arrived two years prior. Since then, I have developed health software for cell phones, which fortunately was adopted by the country I am from. The profits are returned to a scholarship fund that benefits students in my hometown. I speak multiple languages, collaborate with people from different regions, and hear amazing stories about God worldwide.

Today I realize I can help make this crumbling world better! I have not doubted God's blessings, as these are things I couldn't have accomplished on my own. Thank you, God, for not answering my prayer to die in a car accident when I was twelve!

Sometimes, God doesn't give us what we ask for because He doesn't provide us with something that will destroy us. I wish I could end this story with a definitive statement, "I have fully found joy and love from God," but the truth is, I am still growing toward that day by day. Through journaling my prayers, I am finding greater peace and direction for this life God has given me.

My American host mom, Mindy O'Connor, said to me once, "The teacher is always silent while the student is taking a test." Sometimes God's silence means He's watching over us as we are tested.

"She is clothed with strength and dignity; she can laugh at the days to come." (Prov. 31:25 NIV)

ABOUT THE AUTHOR

I haven't always been a pastor's wife, but I have spent most of my adult years seeking God's plan and purpose for my life. My first ministry-related job was working for the National Network of Youth Ministries in San Diego, California.

Everything I did and had done up to that point equipped me for where I am today. Each job I had seemed to be another stepping stone leading me closer and closer to the work I have loved most—serving God and the church.

While still in high school, I began working for the *Visalia Times-Delta* newspaper in the display advertising department. I fell in love with journalism, creating newspaper ads, and working with advertisers from the community and the various departments within the newspaper industry.

During the three years I worked for the *Times-Delta*, I loved the high energy and creativity of working alongside a sales team and graphic artists creating eye-catching ads. Being an extrovert, I loved getting paid to talk to people! It was a trait that served me well in sales and advertising.

After I was married, that trait landed me another great job, working for a flight school and charter service at the San Luis Obispo airport in California. Working with pilots, scheduling their students' flight lessons, and arranging charter flights for people on the Central Coast was also ideally suited for me. One of the best perks of working for a flight school was the free flying lessons I enjoyed.

While interviewing with a company in San Diego, I was given a pre-employment test to determine my strengths and personality traits. When they told me the examination revealed me to be a teacher/counselor, I said, "Great, I'm neither of those." But when my school principal told me she couldn't train her teachers to do what I did naturally, I realized there is a difference between being born with certain gifts, talents, and abilities, and being trained for something.

I began to see patterns in my life that guided me beyond my limitations into possibilities and opportunities I had only once dreamed of. Those experiences eventually led me to nine of the most gratifying years working for a Christian school when doors were supernaturally opened for me to work with kindergarten through high school students. Many of whom referred to me as their school mom.

After working in the computer lab and assisting teachers, I was hired to teach junior-high and high-school journalism, cooking, food prep, and nutrition classes, and running a small on-campus café called The Mega Byte Café. Those years working in Christian education was another stepping stone that led me to become a ministry wife alongside my pastor husband for the past eighteen years.

Writing a book has become a natural next step in sharing my faith journey to encourage others who may be beginning to take their own steps of faith. Maybe you are transitioning from one season of your life to another, wondering how you will make it. My experiences with God will encourage you as you pray for direction and strength to overcome obstacles or setbacks—which we all experience at one time or another. I believe your best is yet to come!

After eleven years of being an international host mom to junior-high and high-school students from China, Vietnam, Korea, and Tanzania, Africa, I now enjoy writing, cooking, hospitality, gardening, and playing with my grandchildren. Currently, I do desktop publishing and serve in various ways behind the scenes as the pastor's wife at the ARK Church in Redlands, California. I can be reached at Mkoconnor910@gmail.com or on Facebook: Mindy Bunting O'Connor Author's Page.

Made in the USA
Las Vegas, NV
16 March 2025